# Haunted
~ *Places* ~
*of*
# Dorset

On the Trail of the Paranormal

## Rupert Matthews

COUNTRYSIDE BOOKS
NEWBURY BERKSHIRE

# •Contents•

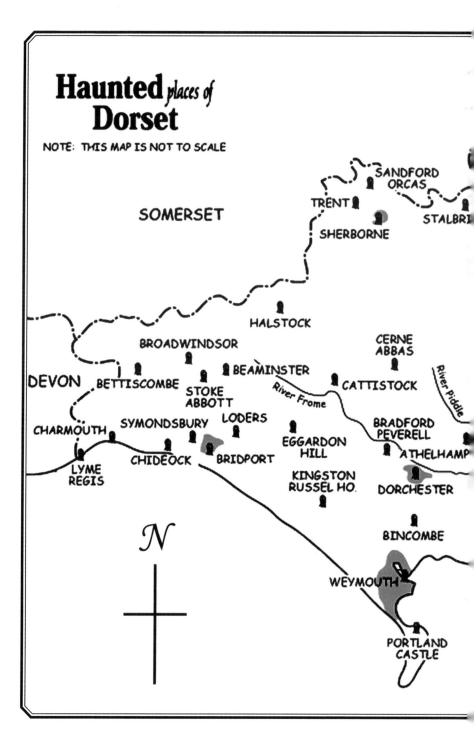

# Haunted *places of* Dorset

NOTE: THIS MAP IS NOT TO SCALE

SOMERSET

SANDFORD ORCAS

TRENT

STALBRI

SHERBORNE

HALSTOCK

BROADWINDSOR

CERNE ABBAS

DEVON

BETTISCOMBE

BEAMINSTER

STOKE ABBOTT

River Frome

CATTISTOCK

River Piddle

CHARMOUTH

SYMONDSBURY

LODERS

BRADFORD PEVERELL

ATHELHAMP

CHIDEOCK

BRIDPORT

EGGARDON HILL

LYME REGIS

KINGSTON RUSSEL HO.

DORCHESTER

BINCOMBE

$N$

WEYMOUTH

PORTLAND CASTLE

4

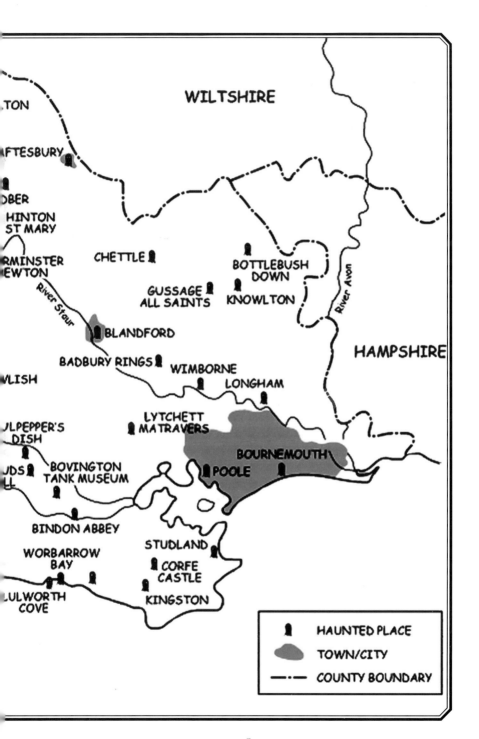

WILTSHIRE

...TON

...FTESBURY

...DBER

HINTON
ST MARY

...RMINSTER
...EWTON

CHETTLE

BOTTLEBUSH
DOWN

GUSSAGE
ALL SAINTS

KNOWLTON

River Stour

River Avon

HAMPSHIRE

BLANDFORD

BADBURY RINGS

WIMBORNE

...LISH

LONGHAM

LYTCHETT
MATRAVERS

...LPEPPER'S
DISH

BOURNEMOUTH

...DS
...LL

BOVINGTON
TANK MUSEUM

POOLE

BINDON ABBEY

STUDLAND

WORBARROW
BAY

CORFE
CASTLE

LULWORTH
COVE

KINGSTON

| | HAUNTED PLACE |
| | TOWN/CITY |
| —·— | COUNTY BOUNDARY |

5

# • Introduction •

Are there such things as ghosts? Many would doubt it, but probably not after they had visited the *Haunted Places of Dorset*.

And Dorset has as wide a range of phantoms, spooks and spectres to offer as any county in England. There is the ancient horseman who gallops over Bottlebush Down, near Gussage All Saints. He has been riding there for some 3,000 years or more, angrily threatening intruders with his axe, and vanishing beside the prehistoric barrow where his bones lie buried. Other ghosts are more modern, as is the White Lady of Charmouth, who has given more than one motorist a bit of a fright.

Some ghosts are enigmatic in the extreme. The ghostly dancers that move across the sands of Lulworth Cove seem to come from the sea and to return there when their macabre dance is finished. Who they are and what their purpose might be is unknown. Equally obscure is the Grey Lady who frequents the White Hart at Sturminster Newton. She appears and disappears for no known reason.

I enjoyed my time travelling around this most lovely of English counties while tracking down the ghosts, spectres and others that fill the pages of this book. The scenery is lovely and the people most welcoming. I would like to thank all those who helped me with my quest for finding the active ghosts of Dorset. The owners of pubs, hotels and other buildings were unfailingly generous with their time and support. Passers-by helped me locate the correct spot on roads and countryside. And above all I must thank my wife for her patience and my little daughter Bo for her distractions.

Rupert Matthews

# • West Dorset •

## SHAFTESBURY

The hilltop town of Shaftesbury began as a fortified settlement built by King Alfred the Great as a bastion against the Viking invasions of the 9th century. He later gave the place to a convent and his own daughter, Ethelgiva, was its first abbess. Thereafter the town kept its royal and sacred connections for centuries and it remained one of the most important places in the county.

The oldest ghosts of Shaftesbury are linked to this era. Walking slowly up the steep cobbled street known as Gold Hill come two phantom men leading a ghostly packhorse on which is slung a human body wrapped in old sacking. These ghosts are more than 1,000 years old, so they can perhaps be forgiven for being rather shadowy and insubstantial when seen. They are recreating the arrival in Shaftesbury of the body of King Edward the Martyr in AD 978. The 18-year-old king was murdered on

*Gold Hill at Shaftesbury has a pair of ghosts more than a thousand years old.*

the orders of his stepmother Elfrida, at Corfe Castle – see the entry on Corfe Castle for details of the crime.

Elfrida needed to get rid of the royal body as quickly as possible and with the minimum of fuss, but could not afford to be accused of treating it with contempt. So she had it carried on horseback to the famous royal convent of Shaftesbury for burial. Edward was later venerated as a martyr and miracles were worked at his tomb in Shaftesbury. The tomb has long gone, but the ghostly re-enactment of his arrival here continues.

The convent survived and prospered and it is a holy resident of the establishment that causes the second haunting of the town. In the

A modern carved stone cross marks the site of the old abbey at Shaftesbury. The few remaining ruins are open to the public only intermittently.

1540s, Henry VIII was busily closing down the monastic houses of England for religious and financial reasons. Despite its ancient claims to royal patronage, Shaftesbury Abbey was to be no exception. The abbess of the time was not one to take things lying down, however. When Abbess Elizabeth Souche heard that the king's men were approaching, she decided to take action. She was hoping that Protestantism might not prove to be a permanent change in England, nor might the closure of her abbey.

Abbess Souche decided therefore to hide the most precious relics and treasures of Shaftesbury Abbey in the hope that one day they could be restored to the abbey when it reopened.

None of the nuns was strong

enough to carry away the treasure, so Abbess Souche gave the task to one of the lay brothers who worked at the heavier chores of the house. The man lifted a large sack of precious relics onto his shoulder and slipped out of the building with a spade as evening fell. He was back at dawn, his mission completed. When the king's men came they closed down the abbey, confiscated its lands and property and packed off Abbess Souche and her nuns with a small pension on which to survive.

*Shaftesbury's Grosvenor Hotel has two phantoms lurking within its walls.*

The months passed and became years, but there was no sign of the king relenting. Then Abbess Souche received a hurrying messenger. The lay brother was ill and needed to talk to her. He died before she reached him and with him died the secret of where the Abbey treasure lay buried. Clearly he died in some distress for his ghost returns frequently to Abbey Walk, the site of the old abbey that he served so faithfully in life.

The phantom monk of Shaftesbury, as the lay brother is called, walks along the wide path without hesitation, then turns off to clamber down the steep slope of the hill that drops down from the public gardens now covering the site. In 1926 a woman saw him as she went to do her shopping in the town. 'He wore a brown cowl and habit,' she reported. 'He came through the wall from the site of the old abbey, crossed the path and then just vanished.' A few people who see him have tried to follow in the hopes that the ghost will lead them to the buried treasure, but nobody is ever able to keep up with the spectral figure as it slides down the slope.

The lost treasure of Shaftesbury will probably remain lost for a good few years yet.

Another ghostly monk lurks at the Grosvenor Hotel, just to the north of the site of the old abbey. Although the hotel itself is about three centuries old, the cellars are much older and are thought to have belonged to the Abbey. This would make sense for it is here that the phantom monk is seen. He does not seem to be a bother to anyone, simply appearing from nowhere to spend a few seconds pottering about on business of his own before vanishing again.

The hotel has a second spectral visitor. This is a lady in a long grey dress who wanders about upstairs looking rather distressed and upset. If anyone tries to offer a word of sympathy, however, she vanishes.

# TODBER

The best known phantom apparition of Todber began to appear in the 1870s, and continues to be seen quite regularly. This is the spectral funeral led by two men carrying a coffin on their shoulders who, most unusually, walk away from the churchyard. One woman who saw the ghosts in the 1920s said: 'I did not see the whole funeral as some have reported. I saw only the men carrying the coffin. There was a black cloth spread over it, which fell down to cover the heads of the men, so that I could not see their faces. The whole thing was come and gone in a trice.'

The apparition began to be seen only after workmen at a quarry to the east of the village uncovered a large quantity of human bones as they opened up a new section of stone. Rumours at once abounded that a battle had been fought on the site many generations earlier. It was never entirely clear when the battle had been fought nor, indeed, if anyone had heard of the battle before the skeletons were found.

There are those who believe that it would be unlikely for pallbearers to carry a coffin from the village to a battlefield for burial. It would be more likely that the dead were pushed into a mass grave and any wounded who died later would have been interred in the churchyard. Perhaps the ghosts point to a different explanation. In the 1340s the Black Death struck Dorset especially hard. It might be more likely that the mass of ancient bones were buried in a plague pit, where the bodies of the wretched victims of the epidemic were hurriedly interred at a safe distance from the village where the risk of contagion was slight. If so, the ghosts are those of mourners attending a funeral for a plague victim.

Less uncertainty surrounds the ghost that frequented a cottage in the village. The figure of a man in a long coat with brass buttons and pale breeches used to be seen quite often. The spectre was easily recognised as that of a former occupant of the cottage who had died in the 18th century. The place was pulled down in the later Victorian era, and a small chest of gold coins was found hidden beneath the hearthstone. The ghost was never seen again, so it was widely believed that it had been guarding the treasure that it had hoarded in life.

## Hinton St Mary

The ghost at Hinton St Mary is a shadowy visitor, but one that manages to be both ancient and modern at the same time. For generations nothing particularly odd happened at Hinton St Mary. Then a man, doing some otherwise harmless digging in his garden beside the B3092, turned up some mosaic tiles. Archaeologists were called and a dig organised. A small Roman villa was discovered. It was nothing fancy, in many ways not much more than a large farmhouse. But it must have been the beloved home of somebody all those centuries ago.

Soon after the excavations were completed and the archaeologists departed, a strange figure began to be seen in the area. Tall and dressed in a long pale cloak, the apparition flitted about the roadside close to the site of the villa. One person who saw him described the clothing as being a toga, so the figure was instantly taken to be the ghost of a Roman disturbed by the digging.

Whether this shadowy figure in his swirling cloak is a Roman ghost or not, he seems to be fading. He has not been seen much in recent years so perhaps he is retreating back to wherever he came from now that his beloved home is undisturbed once again.

## STURMINSTER NEWTON

Time was when Sturminster Newton was famous for hosting the most important livestock market in Dorset. These days it is better known as a centre from which tourists can explore the charming Blackmoor Vale, with its good walking paths, fine coarse fishing and secluded villages. Most visitors are attracted by the olde worlde quaintness of the place and do not realise that the town is, by Dorset standards, fairly modern. In 1729 a fire broke out after a long dry spell of hot summer weather and almost the entire town burned down. What is seen today dates from the rebuilding of the 1730s.

Only two buildings survived intact. The first was the church, now noted for its fine Victorian stained glass. The second was the White Hart Inn, noted for its welcoming ales and its ghost. The ghostly resident is an enigmatic lady, who is seen walking around the bar area on the ground floor. Nobody knows who she was when alive nor why she frequents the White Hart, but she does not seem to be any real trouble.

Across the market place stands the Swan Inn, rebuilt after the fire on the site of a much older hostelry. This pub is haunted by a landlord who ran the inn in the 1790s. Although he was a famously jovial host, the man had some dark secret that caused him to hang himself in the cellar one night.

The 'Old Boy', as the ghost has become known, was soon active in the pub. He appeared, as he did in life, as a rather rotund and cheerful looking man, dressed in a dark suit with what may be an apron round

*Sturminster Newton's White Hart is haunted by a quiet and inoffensive phantom..*

his waist. He is seen most often near the stairs that lead up to the private areas of the pub, and sometimes on the stairs as well. One customer who saw the ghost in the 1990s while on the way to the gents' toilet mistook him for another customer on the same errand. He followed the figure round a corner, to find the spectre had vanished completely. There was nowhere for him to have gone, other than the gents, but he was not there. 'It fair took my mind off the business in hand,' said the witness.

Sturminster Newton stands in a loop of the River Stour, with bridges to the south and west. That to the south is medieval in date and carries motor traffic; the Colber Bridge to the west is Victorian and caters for pedestrians only. It is the Colber Bridge that is haunted. The bridge leads to open fields where once stood the medieval village of Colber, of which only a single farm built in the 18th century remains.

This farm, Plumber Manor, is now a restaurant, but in the 18th century it was home to a squire who was absolutely devoted to fox hunting. He rode to hounds whenever he could, even neglecting the business of running his estates. Such a devotion to sport made Squire

Plumber popular locally, though the brutality with which he would treat his horse and hounds was not so well thought of. If his horse refused a jump it would get a sound whipping, if his hounds failed to kill a fox, they were thoroughly beaten.

On one fatal day no fox was found and Squire Plumber returned home in a bad mood. Leaping down from his horse, he grabbed a coach whip and advanced on his pack of hounds. But this time the dogs did not cower, instead they snarled, growled and then pounced on their tormentor. Squire Plumber fled, racing north over the fields towards Colber Bridge and what he hoped would be the safety of Sturminster Newton. He never made it.

Just as he approached the bridge, Squire Plumber was brought down by his dogs and torn to pieces. The grisly events are played out in spectral form to this day. Seen from Colber Bridge, the figure of a tall, muscular man in hunting kit comes running over the fields pursued by a pack of hounds. As the strange hunt reaches the bridge, the man falls and all the spectral figures vanish.

*The Colber Bridge at Sturminster Newton gives access to some very haunted fields beyond the river.*

# STALBRIDGE MANOR

The story of the haunting of Stalbridge Manor was a classic ghost story of the Victorian era. Although it is impossible today to decide how much of the tale is true – the house long having been demolished – it remains one of the most often quoted tales of the supernatural in Dorset.

The account begins when a Mrs M. (19th-century accounts were often infuriatingly anonymous to protect the reputations of the witnesses) rented the Jacobean Stalbridge Manor for the summer. The owner of the house told her that she had to obey any instructions given her by the housekeeper, who was to remain on site throughout the rental period.

When Mrs M. arrived, the housekeeper duly gave her various instructions about the care of the house and its contents. Rather bizarrely, she also told Mrs M. that she must not use the Great Hall in the afternoon and must on no account be in the room at 5 pm. For several weeks all was well. Then Mrs M. invited some local boys and girls to spend the day at the manor to play with her own children. The day went well and as the afternoon drew to a close Mrs M. saw the children off from the front door. It was only as she turned to walk back across the Great Hall that she realised the time. A clock chimed five.

Instantly a door at the top of the stairs flew open and an elderly woman came running out engulfed in flames and screaming, 'I have done it'. The startling apparition then vanished abruptly. Rather shaken, Mrs M. decided to quit the house at once. Some time later she chanced to meet the owner of the house at a social event and felt she should explain why she had abandoned the lease so suddenly.

The owner nodded grimly and told Mrs M. the story behind the haunting. Back in the early 18th century the house was in the hands of an elderly widow and her only son. The boy fell in love with the pretty daughter of a servant and wanted to marry her. His mother refused to give her permission to her son marrying so far beneath him. When the boy went ahead with the wedding anyway, his mother threw him out. Some months later the old woman seemed to relent and invited her son and daughter-in-law to return to live at Stalbridge Manor. All appeared well, but one day the husband came home to find his wife had died, her long cotton dress having accidentally caught fire after sweeping into a fireplace. The man was distraught and organised a grand funeral. As the years passed he remarried and brought up a family.

It was not until many years later, as his mother lay dying, that the man learned the awful truth. His mother had been determined to get rid of the servant girl-cum-wife and had taken advantage of being alone with her one afternoon to push her into the fireplace and so cause her death.

*The stone lions that guard the entrance to Stalbridge Park are said to come to life on certain nights and spring down from their plinths to prowl the area.*

It was the ghost of the wicked mother that was thereafter seen at 5 pm, the time of the dreadful crime, emerging from the room in which she had killed her unwanted daughter-in-law.

The ghost vanished when the house was demolished, but supernatural activity remains. The entrance to Stalbridge Park is flanked by two massive gateposts, on top of which are carved magnificent lions. According to local legend, these lions climb down from their pillars on the stroke of midnight to drink at a nearby pond. And woe betide anyone who is in the vicinity at the time, for the lions are notoriously ill-tempered and are prone to attack anyone to whom they take a dislike.

# SANDFORD ORCAS

The manor at Sandford Orcas entered the news headlines when it became the centre of a heated dispute over ghosts in 1966. Earlier that year the BBC had broadcast a programme about haunted houses and had named Sandford Orcas Manor as having a strong reputation for being haunted.

The programme spurred Mr A. Medlycott of Cranborne, who had lived in the house from 1916 to 1964, to contact the press and vehemently deny that his old home was haunted. 'During the whole of that time,' he wrote in a letter published in the Western Gazette, 'no ghosts were seen nor were any unusual sounds or happenings noticed by either the family or their guests, or staff. Had there, in fact, been any tales of ghosts there would have been no reason to suppress them, though doubtless they would not have been communicated to the press.'

*The presence, or not, of ghosts at Sandford Orcas Manor has been the subject of much debate, but there can be no denying the persistent stories about the place.*

This prompted a letter from a Miss M. Gallo who was the daughter of servants of the Medlycott family. She had lived as a child in a small apartment on the top floor and recalled, 'We often heard knocking on the doors, windows opening and closing and curtains being drawn back and forward. At the time my parents didn't believe us as we were small. I was six-years-old and my sister was five.'

Of rather more import was the intervention of Colonel and Mrs Claridge, the then owners of the manor. They reported that the house was definitely haunted. Mrs Claridge had seen the phantom of an elderly lady in a red dress walk up the stairs from the Great Hall and enter a bedroom. When Mrs Claridge followed, the room was empty although there was only the one door. Another member of the family had seen a woman in Elizabethan dress, complete with starched collar, walk out of the manor and across the courtyard before vanishing abruptly.

To sort the matter out, Colonel Claridge invited a team of three researchers from the Paraphysical Laboratory to visit and investigate. Armed with temperature gauges, cameras, recorders and a host of other equipment, the three came and stayed for some time. When they left, Mr Benson Herbert, the team leader, announced that the building was quite definitely haunted, but was not willing to state specifically by whom.

In the years since, the manor's reputation has grown by leaps and bounds. Among the figures reported are a ghostly monk, a lady in a green dress and a man dressed in velvet. Most dramatic is the tall footman whose appearances are always accompanied by a putrid and disgusting smell. He is rumoured to have been an 18th-century servant who raped a maid and was packed off to prison where he died. Rather more precise is the identification of the spectral man in a smock, who is seen in and around the kitchen, as James Davidge. This farmer rented the manor in the early 1740s, but got into financial difficulties and hanged himself in the kitchen.

By comparison the ghost that appears at the nearby church is rather prosaic. This man appears to run up the central aisle with a large key in his hand. He is seen for only a few steps at a time before he vanishes as abruptly as he appeared.

## TRENT

The B3148 runs north-west out of Sherborne to cross Charlock Hill on its way to Shepton Mallet. Today it is a fairly safe road, but this was not always the case. Charlock Hill is both high and steep. It has been necessary to hack cuttings out of the hill to enable the road to reach the summit on a fairly even track before dropping down the northern side of the hill.

Before the cuttings were made the northern slope was famously difficult to negotiate with horse-drawn carts or carriages. The spot beside Trent Barrow had a particularly bad reputation. It was here in the 1780s that a coach and four racing north from Sherborne came to grief. It is thought that the horses and brakes were unable to keep the coach to a sensible speed as it went down the hill. The driver could not control the careering vehicle, which came off the road near Trent Barrow, overturned and killed everyone on board.

To this day the ghostly coach recreates the accident in horrific detail. It comes tearing down the hill to the sound of screaming voices and thundering hooves. The coach then smashes off the road, overturns and vanishes.

## SHERBORNE

Sherborne Castle was begun in the later 11th century by a Norman nobleman named Osmond, who later gave it to the Bishops of Salisbury. When he made the gift, Osmond laid a solemn curse upon it. The documents record him as saying, 'Whosoever shall take those lands from the bishopric or diminish them in great or small, should be accursed, not only in this world but also in the world to come; unless in his lifetime he make restitution thereof.'

Whether it was the curse, the strength of the fortifications or some other cause, the castle had a remarkably quiet history for a military

*The Elizabethan courtier Sir Walter Raleigh haunts his old home at Sherborne.*

building. However, when the Reformation of the 16th century swept away the monasteries and stripped many bishoprics of their more profitable holdings, the lands of Sherborne were taken from the Church and handed to the enthusiastically Protestant Edward Seymour, Duke of Somerset, by the equally Protestant King Edward VI. Soon the curse seemed to be working for in 1552 Edward VI tired of Somerset's ambition and had him executed. The estate was taken by the young king, who promptly died of consumption the following year.

The Sherborne lands then passed to the new monarch, the Catholic Mary I, who kept hold of the estates, and could be said to have made restitution by paying money to the Church in recompense for some of what was lost in the Reformation. She died childless and so the throne passed to her younger sister, Elizabeth I. Elizabeth in turn leased the estates and castle to her favourite, Sir Walter Raleigh, at a tiny rent.

Raleigh loved the place, but found the old castle too draughty and chilly for his taste. He began building what is known today as the New Castle, though it is really a lovely Tudor mansion rather than a castle. Raleigh too seemed to have evaded the curse – at first. He grew wealthy on government contracts and appointments, was elected to Parliament and was recognised as one of the most influential men in government. He sent naval expeditions to the Americas and is credited with introducing potatoes and tobacco to England. It was at Sherborne that Raleigh was enjoying a quiet pipe of tobacco when a servant, thinking his employer was on fire, threw a bucket of water over him.

Such good fortune did not last. In March 1603 Queen Elizabeth died and with her went Raleigh's influence at court. He failed to support King James of Scotland, who inherited the crown of England, and so earned that monarch's hatred. In 1616 Raleigh led a naval expedition to South America that went badly wrong, ending with serious bloodshed in a battle against local Spanish settlers. On his return to England, Raleigh was arrested on the orders of King James, who was as keen to curry favour with Spain as he was to get rid of such an important relic of Elizabeth's court. Raleigh was executed on 29th September 1618.

Almost immediately the ghost of Sir Walter began to be seen in the grounds of Sherborne Castle. Dressed in his splendid court dress of richly decorated doublet and hose, he wandered quietly around the gardens, but was seen most often on a stone seat that today bears his name. The ghost still appears in the grounds, a particularly clear sighting being gained by a workman in 1983. Sir Walter seems to be most active in the autumn, around the anniversary of his execution.

As for the curse, that seems to have died with Raleigh. After his death the lands were acquired by the Digby family, who have enjoyed them ever since.

# HALSTOCK

The legend behind the haunting at Halstock is an ancient one, dating back to the days when Christianity had only recently arrived in Dorset. The pagan gods were still strong, but were on the wane in the face of the true religion. It was this conflict, fought for the great prize of human souls, that came to Halstock some time in the AD 700s.

In those days the richest landowner in Halstock was a Christian man named Benna, who had a beautiful and virtuous daughter named Juthware. Benna's wife had died when Juthware was born and, as the

*The church at Halstock stands on the site of an ancient martyrdom that has left its ghostly traces in the village.*

years passed, he felt that he needed a wife as Juthware needed a mother. Benna's eye fell on a Welsh woman named Goneril – many of the native Britons still lived in Dorset at this time and were generally referred to as Welsh by the English newcomers. Goneril had a son, Bana, who was much the same age as Juthware so the match seemed a sensible one.

Unfortunately, Goneril was more interested in Benna's wealth than in his love. She played the part of a dutiful wife well enough, but secretly she despised the Christian faith of Benna and Juthware. In particular, she disliked the way both were lavish in hospitality and generous in their giving of alms to the poor. Bana was brought up to be a pagan, like his mother, but as the years passed he became increasingly fond of his stepsister and that fondness grew into love.

Time came when Benna died. To Goneril's fury Benna left his entire lands and estates to his daughter, with not a penny nor an acre for his second wife. Juthware proved to be as Christian in her attitude as her father had been, so she allowed her stepmother and stepbrother to live rent free in a cottage on the estates. It was not enough for Goneril, who laid her plans.

Watching the growing love of her son and stepdaughter, Goneril devised a wicked plan. She began to tell Bana that young Juthware was seeing another man – a Christian – and that she would never consent to marry a pagan such as Bana. The boy did not believe his mother's tale, but still jealousy crept into his heart and he began to grow suspicious. When Goneril judged her son's mind was sufficiently full of doubts, she acted. She took a new born lamb into the woods that then covered what is now Abbot's Hill, slit its throat and skinned it.

A modern road name commemorates the ghost that haunts the village of Halstock.

She then hurried to her son to tell him that his beloved Juthware had given birth to an illegitimate child, killed it and thrown the remains in the woods. Bana knew that the child could not be his for Juthware, as a good Christian, had refused his advances until such time as he accepted the new religion so that they might be married. Frantic with jealousy, but equally desperate to believe in the faithfulness of his love, Bana dragged Juthware up to Abbot's Hill to the spot indicated by his mother. There he found the dead, skinned lamb and in a rage of disappointment and anger sliced off Juthware's head with a single blow from his sword.

Instead of falling to the ground, Juthware calmly bent down and picked up her severed head. Carrying the grisly relic before her, she set off down the hill back to Halstock. Quaking with fear and dread, Bana and Goneril followed her. The walking corpse carried its head into Halstock church, laid it on the altar and only then fell dead. Faced by the miracle, Goneril confessed her crimes and proclaimed the girl's innocence. She was swiftly dealt with by the savage justice of the time, while Bana turned Christian, becoming a hermit monk tending a small shrine that he built on the site of Juthware's martyrdom. Juthware was proclaimed a saint and quite a cult of veneration grew up around her at Halstock.

The Reformation swept away the saintly cult of St Juthware, as it did so many others in England. But no amount of religious change could stop her ghost. She walks with stately tread, and carrying her head in her arms, down from Abbot's Hill to the church. Recreating the miraculous walk of all those years ago, the headless saint is seen most often in the autumn, traditionally around early November.

## Cerne Abbas

The most famous feature of the charming village of Cerne Abbas stands just outside the village to the north. This is the famously priapic Cerne Giant chalk figure. The figure is that of a gigantic man striding to his right with an upright club in his right hand. He is completely naked and his male organ is as upright as his club. It is said that postcards of the Cerne Giant are the only pornographic images that the Post Office will handle.

In the village below the giant stands the New Inn, a welcoming pub that belies its name by being one of the older buildings in the village, though one of the less ancient pubs. Until the mid-19th century the New Inn was used as a temporary courthouse whenever the local Justices of the Peace needed a room large enough to try the various cases of theft, poaching or other misdemeanours that came their way. The room in question was towards the back of the pub, while what is now the main bar was used as a waiting room in which witnesses or others could sit to wait their turn in court.

It is generally assumed that the ghost who haunts the bar is one such person, who came here for a court case. Certainly his clothes would date him to the early 19th century. He wears a long jacket or coat over a waistcoat and riding trousers. The man is middle-aged and sits quite patiently with his back to the wall close to the fireplace. He looks up as if his name has been called and walks across the bar to pass through the door and into a corridor that leads to where the court used to sit. He never reaches the end of the corridor, but always vanishes part way along it.

Who he was and what the result of his case might have been, nobody knows. He just returns time and again to sit in the bar, then walks off to whatever duty calls him.

The rear garden of the New Inn is haunted by quite different ghosts. These are the bright, cheerful phantoms of a pair of young children who run about laughing and playing quite happily. The two girls are dressed in summer frocks, and it is this that gives away their supernatural status for they may be seen at any time of year, and running about in cotton dresses is not usual for mortals in the depths of winter.

Who these ghosts are is obscure, as is their link – if any – with the famous giant that looks down upon them.

---

*The New Inn at Cerne Abbas has at least two ghosts and a fine selection of meals to tempt the visitor.*

## DEWLISH

Dewlish is a fairly small village off the beaten track to the north-east of Dorchester. It stands astride the ominously named Devil's Brook, but it is not the evil one who haunts the place.

The ghost here is a rather sad individual named Betsey Caine. She was a farmgirl who hanged herself in around 1830, apparently as a result of a love affair gone wrong. In those unforgiving times suicides were not permitted a church burial, so the mortal remains of poor Betsey Caine were taken off to a patch of woodland on her father's farm and buried quietly and secretly among the trees.

It was not long before villagers began to see Betsey Caine again. Her ghost took to sitting on the gate that led into the woodland where she was buried. Soon the lane passing the gate, which led to Milborne St Andrew, came to be avoided after dark. The unfortunate Betsey Caine can be seen there yet. But passing motorists will have to be quick, for the spot is on a corner and sweeping headlights pass it in an instant.

## ATHELHAMPTON HALL

It was in 1485 that Sir William Martyn, Lord Mayor of London and fabulously wealthy merchant, decided that the time had come to find a rural retreat for himself and his family. He found Athelhampton, a mile east of Puddletown, and set about building himself a house of impressive design. Today it is home to ghosts both human and animal.

The Wars of the Roses had just come to a bloody end at Bosworth Field, where King Richard III was killed and the Crown seized by Henry Tudor. Henry energetically imposed peace on England, crushing any nobleman who showed signs of causing trouble and keeping the country free of booty-hungry brigands. Thus it was that Martyn was able to

*Athelhampton Hall was built at the end of the Wars of the Roses for a rich City of London merchant who wished to retire to the country.*

abandon the fortifications that had been necessary on earlier houses. Instead of stout walls and tall towers, Martyn's house boasted large windows and carved decorations. He included a few battlements for the sake of show, but they were just decoration.

Martyn's family emblem was a monkey looking into a mirror, a motif that is repeated in stone and stained glass at several points around the house. He also had a pet monkey, and subsequent generations of the family continued the tradition. In 1595 the last male descendant of the family lay dying. His pet monkey came into the room as if to view its master on his deathbed. As the man breathed his last, the monkey let out a scream and bolted from the room. It was never seen again, but ever since then the sound of scratching has been heard coming from behind the panelling in the Great Hall. It is generally reckoned to be the phantom sound of the monkey.

The scratching monkey is not the only ghost in the Great Hall. This chamber was built to impress, with its linen-fold panelling, massive wooden ceiling and heraldic motifs. It was here that successive owners welcomed guests and entertained in grand fashion. It was here, also, that a local gentleman of Royalist persuasions got into an argument with a fellow who preferred the cause of Parliament in the tense months that led up to the English Civil War of the 1640s. The men drew their swords and fought a dramatic battle around the room. The duel ended in wounds, not death, but it has left its ghostly mark. The two men have been seen, thrusting and hacking with their swords around the room. The fight continues until one inflicts on the other a slashing wound down the right arm, at which point the duellists fade from view.

Seen almost as rarely is the ghostly cooper who works down in the cellars. Hammering away at a barrel with a mallet, the man is clearly intent on his task and pays no attention to any humans who wander into his domain.

A rather more active ghost frequents the State Bedroom. This impressive yet rather cosy room is kept in splendid 16th-century fashion. The ghost who strides through, walking towards the Yellow Room, must feel quite at home. Although nobody knows whose ghost this is, her clothes are clearly of 16th-century date. Dressed in a dark grey gown, the lady moves with silent, but determined pace.

Once, some 80 years ago, a housemaid was doing some cleaning in the State Bedroom when she saw a figure enter the room from the corner of her eye. Thinking it to be a fellow servant, the maid called out, 'I am cleaning in here. You can make yourself useful elsewhere.' Imagine her surprise when the newcomer promptly vanished into thin air.

*Athelhampton's State Bedroom is home to a ghostly lady dressed in fashions of 16th-century date.*

## DORCHESTER

One of the best recorded ghosts in Dorset haunts, or perhaps haunted, St Peter's church in High West Street. The ghost first appeared in dramatic fashion on Christmas Eve, 1814. The popular and long-serving vicar, Reverend Nathaniel Templeman, had passed away a few months earlier and the new vicar had left the task of decorating the church for Christmas Day to his sexton, Ambrose Hunt and warden, Clerk Hardy.

The two men were skilled and dedicated, so after some hours of work in the chilly church they had a fine display ready for the parish's devotions the following day. The two men were understandably tired, so they decided to refresh themselves with a glass of the communion wine that they knew to be in the vestry. They poured themselves a generous glass each and retired to sit down on a pew to enjoy the drink.

*St Peter's church in Dorchester is frequented by the phantom of a former vicar. By all accounts he does not seem a particularly happy ghost.*

At that moment the ghost of the Rev. Templeman suddenly appeared coming towards them. The phantom was obviously angry, waving his fists and mouthing as if shouting, though no sound could be heard. As the ghost drew close, Hardy collapsed in a faint. Hunt threw himself to his knees and began reciting the Lord's Prayer. The ghost paused, then turned aside and drifted off down the north aisle, where it vanished. As soon as the ghost had gone, Hunt leapt

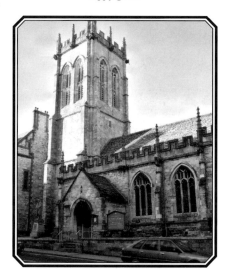

*Now the Judge Jeffreys Restaurant, this house in Dorchester was the residence of that notorious lawyer when he stayed in the town. His brief visit has left its phantom mark here.*

to his feet and fled into the night. He barged into a nearby inn and gabbled out his story. A few of the more intrepid souls in the bar hurried to the church. They found the unfortunate Hardy lying unconscious on the floor and the two glasses of communion wine overturned, but of the ghost there was no sign.

The ghostly vicar is said to have returned several times since, always in apparent anger. But none of these reports are as well attested as that of the sexton and warden. They, after all, knew the dead man well and encountered his ghost at a range of only 10 feet or so. They were adamant about what they had seen and never changed their story.

On the opposite side of the road from the church and just uphill a few steps is the Judge Jeffreys Restaurant. This place takes its name from Judge George Jeffreys, the 17th-century judge usually remembered as 'the infamous Jeffreys'. After a promising career as a civil lawyer, Jeffreys had turned to criminal law and earned himself a fearsome reputation as a prosecutor who was none too scrupulous about how he gained a conviction. Rumours of hiring false witnesses or bribing jurors began to cluster around Jeffreys, but powerful patrons protected him. Chief among these was James, Duke of York, brother to King Charles II. When James came to the throne as King James II, he made Jeffreys Lord

Chancellor with instructions to crack down on any Protestants who objected to the new king's open Catholicism.

In 1685 the dashing, handsome and very Protestant Duke of Monmouth raised a rebellion against James II. Monmouth landed at Lyme Regis and many Dorset men joined the swelling ranks of his army. However, modern weaponry meant that hastily trained country lads were no match for royal troops armed with muskets, cannon and armour. At Sedgemoor in Somerset, Monmouth was defeated. King James gave Jeffreys the task of acting as judge at the following trials of the rebels.

Jeffreys soon showed himself to be a particularly ruthless, merciless and unscrupulous judge. He refused to hear witnesses whose evidence he did not like, would not allow the accused to speak and threatened jurors that they would be treated as rebels themselves if they did not convict the accused. All those with the slightest connection to Monmouth and his rising were convicted of treason and hundreds were sent to the gallows. Finally the public outcry at Jeffreys' behaviour forced James to halt the hangings, the surviving convicts being sold as slaves in the West Indies instead.

It was a brutal time for Dorset, and Dorchester did not escape. Jeffreys stayed in the house that is now the restaurant named after him, hearing the cases brought before him in the main function room of the Antelope Inn around the corner. None of these unfortunates escaped the rope and, to make doubly certain the lesson was not lost on the good citizens of Dorchester, Jeffreys had the severed heads of his victims spiked on the railings around St Peter's church.

Perhaps it is no wonder that the restaurant is said to be haunted by those sent to their deaths by the heartless Jeffreys. Rather more surprising, however, is the fact that Jeffreys himself is said to haunt the shopping arcade that now occupies the old Antelope Inn. His figure emerges from a door that leads to the house where he stayed, turns left down the arcade and then vanishes beside what was the entrance to the room where he held his trials. Jeffreys does not seem to have had an uneasy conscience, so it is not clear why his ghost lurks here.

A little further up the hill is the Royal Wessex Hotel. The phantom here is seen quite often, but only ever from outside the building. She is dressed in a bonnet that may date her to the early Victorian period. Always her behaviour is the same, she looks out of a window on the ground floor, scanning the faces of passers-by as if seeking somebody in particular. After a few seconds she vanishes from sight.

At the top of High West Street a turning on the right leads to The West Walks. This raised footpath runs along what was formerly the embankment on which stood the Roman fortifications of Durnovaria, the Roman city that stood on this site. Along this walk has been seen pacing a rather sad apparition wearing armour and carrying a shield. He is said to be a Roman legionary on patrol along his old route.

To the west of the town stands the impressive Wolveton House. This grand house is on the site of a fortified manor house that dates back to around the year AD 850. That first house was torn down in the 1530s by Thomas Trenchard, but he left the 14th-century gatehouse to be part of the new house he built. This structure was, in turn, reconstructed in the 1630s by Sir George Trenchard. The house fell into neglect after the Trenchards moved to a more modern residence, but has now been handsomely restored by the present owners, relatives of the Trenchards, and is open to the public.

The oldest of the various ghosts of Wolveton dates back to 1594. Sir George Trenchard was the Justice of the Peace at the time, so it fell to him to deal with an Irishman named Cornelius. This Cornelius was a Catholic priest who had been arrested at Chideock. Unlike some of the more fanatical Catholics sent from Rome, Cornelius did not seem intent on either the murder of the Protestant Queen Elizabeth I nor on stirring up religious hatred and causing riots and bloodshed. He seemed more concerned with baptising the children of the few remaining Catholics still living in Dorset.

Nevertheless, Cornelius was a Catholic priest who had entered England without permission. Sir George locked the man up in the gatehouse of Wolveton, giving him a comfortable room on the first floor

*The ghostly Cornelius haunts the gatehouse towers of Wolveton House,
where he was imprisoned.*

of the south tower, and sent a message to London asking for advice on how to proceed. After some weeks, word came back that Cornelius was to be sent to London for questioning. What those questions were, and how Cornelius responded, we do not know for the records have been lost. But the government in London suddenly pronounced the man guilty of treason and sent him to Dorchester together with orders for instant execution. The Irish priest was hanged on 3rd July 1594.

Soon afterwards footsteps began to be heard moving around the chambers so recently vacated by the luckless Cornelius. His tread can be heard still, from time to time, pacing restlessly back and forth.

Just as unnerving was the apparition that appeared in the 1630s. Sir

Thomas Trenchard was hosting a formal dinner for the local magistrates on the occasion of the Judges of Assize visiting Dorchester to conduct a series of trials. A few minutes after the company sat down to dine, one of the judges leapt to his feet. His face had suddenly gone pale and he appeared to have trouble talking. After a few seconds he beckoned his servant over and demanded that his carriage be got ready. Without pausing to wish Sir Thomas goodnight, the judge grabbed his hat and fled into the night.

The judge ordered the driver to take him to a clergyman, and poured out a bizarre tale. He said that as he sat down, he chanced to glance over towards Lady Trenchard. Behind the lady's chair stood a phantom of Lady Trenchard with a cut throat and blood pumping from the wound. As soon as he leapt to his feet, the apparition had gone. Imagine the man's feelings when a messenger arrived next day to announce that Lady Trenchard had committed suicide in the night by cutting her throat.

However, by far the most famous and spectacular ghost of Wolveton dates to the 1730s. At some point in that decade, nobody seems very clear when, the heir to the estates hosted a dinner that turned out to involve the consumption of rather more wine than was wise. The heir and his companions – as young men do – fell to drunken boasting, in this case about their skills as horsemen. 'Why,' declared the heir, 'I could drive my carriage anywhere most men could walk.' 'Then drive it in here,' came an answering challenge.

The Eating Chamber where the drinking was taking place was on the first floor, at the top of Wolveton's unique Great Staircase. There is no other staircase like this in any house in England. It is wide and broad and built entirely of stone. The pierced balustrade has Romanesque arches, interspersed with carvings of naked women, and ends in a dramatic caryatid or female figure.

Nothing daunted, the young man lurched to the stables and ordered the groom to hitch a horse to his racing carriage. The whip was vigorously applied and the vehicle driven into the house and up the Great Staircase. The horse's hooves clattered and scraped on the stone, but the heir drove it on to drag the carriage up the stairs, then through the doorway flanked by Corinthian columns at the top and into the barrel-vaulted Eating Chamber. The date of 1732 carved into the stone of the Great Staircase is generally reckoned to commemorate the feat.

It is this drunken escapade that is repeated time after time by a phantom carriage, pulled by a great black stallion that is whipped on by a man standing upright by the driving seat. This is a dramatic haunting indeed, but one that is not encountered so often as that of the unfortunate Cornelius.

Originally outside Dorchester, but now in the firm embrace of spreading suburbs and housing estates, stands Maumbury Rings. This edifice is all that remains of the amphitheatre built by the Romans to hold gladiatorial combats, public executions and other shows of typically bloodthirsty taste. The site continued to be used for public hangings until the 18th century, after which executions were held outside Dorchester prison on the other side of town.

It is therefore difficult to date with accuracy the ghosts seen here. They appear for only a moment or two, but in large numbers. A crowd is seen filling the interior slopes and gazing at some spectacle taking place before them. Traditionally the phantoms are said to be Romans watching a gladiator fight, but the descriptions of the ghosts are so vague that this cannot be certain.

Further south from Dorchester, and still outside the modern sprawl of the town, is the dramatic earthwork of Maiden Castle. This was the main stronghold of the Durotriges who ruled the area before the Roman invasion of AD 43. The fortress was stormed by the Roman commander Vespasian, who later became emperor, and the marks of the battle have been uncovered by archaeologists. Once they had taken the place, the Romans were determined that they should never be put to such trouble again. They forced the thousands of inhabitants to move to a less easily defended site in the valley below, which is how the town of Dorchester began. The ghosts seen on Maiden Castle are, however, most definitely Roman, for they have been seen to be wearing togas. No doubt they are associated with the small Roman temple that stood here. Perhaps the new regime wished to placate the old gods, and so allowed their worship to continue on the original site.

# BRADFORD PEVERELL

U pstream from Dorchester, the charming village of Bradford Peverell lies strung out along the banks of the River Frome. It is now bypassed by the modern A37, but the older road from Dorchester, heading north, runs through the village. Sometime around the year 1807, tragedy came to Bradford Peverell along this road.

This was the time when roads across England were being improved and maintained to much higher standards than had previously been the case. The new roads were the delight of wealthy young men who invested in exciting new vehicles known as chaises. These were lightly-built carriages able to hold only two or three people and pulled by a single horse. The light construction and narrow wheels meant that these vehicles could be driven at high speed.

One such chaise driven by a daring young man came racing along the road out of Dorchester and tore up the main street of Bradford Peverell. It dashed past in a flurry of hooves and flying dust on its way towards Muckleford. Then something went wrong. The light carriage skidded sideways, veered off the road and lurched down the slope into the waters of the River Frome. The slope is almost sheer, dropping down as a cliff some 20 feet high. Although the river is not especially wide, it is bordered by extensive marsh and bog, making the going treacherous for any foolish enough to walk this way. The carriage overturned, killing driver and horse in a crash that threw spray far and wide.

This ghastly scene is recreated on the road west of Bradford Peverell once or twice every year, usually on summer's evenings when the warm Dorset sun is dipping down behind the hills above Muckleford, just as it did on that fatal day some two centuries previously.

# CATTISTOCK

Almost two centuries ago there was a supernatural mystery at Cattistock. A phantom man began to be seen in the lanes north of the village. Nobody who saw the spectre recognised him nor could anyone explain why the ghost sometimes called out, 'Search for Wat Perkins'. Who was Wat Perkins? Why was he lost? Nobody had any answers – at least, none that they were willing to admit to.

For more than two decades the enigmatic ghost was seen wandering the area. Then a gang of workmen was put to the task of removing a roadside hedge. They were not from the area and were unfamiliar with the ghostly goings on. They were shocked to find a headless skeleton buried in a shallow grave among the hedge roots. As the men stood wondering what to do, an elderly woman came hurrying over from a nearby cottage. She begged them to rebury the bones and tell no one of the discovery, and offered to pay them handsomely for doing so.

*The lanes north of Cattistock and the local manor were the venue for a spectral mystery that had a gruesome and surprising solution.*

The men were more honest than greedy, so they spurned her money and sent one man off to find the forces of law and order. When the local Justice of the Peace arrived, his first call was on the old woman, Kit Whistle. He found her sitting morosely by her fire. She pointed at the fire. 'The head is under the hearth stone,' she said. Calling in the workmen, the JP quickly got the hearth lifted up and there, sure enough, was the skull missing from the body outside.

It later transpired that Kit Whistle had murdered a man for his money some 20 years earlier. She had been alone at home soon after her husband died when a pedlar came calling. The man was tired and hungry, so she had offered to prepare him a meal in return for a few pennies. But as the man ate, she saw that he had a full purse bulging with gold and silver coins. The pedlar was a stranger with an accent Kit Whistle had never heard before. Clearly he was from many miles away and, she reasoned, would not be missed. When the pedlar lay down to rest, she slit his throat. She then hacked off his head to avoid identification and buried the skull beneath her hearth. That night she dragged the body out and hurriedly buried it beneath the nearby hedge, thinking that it would never be discovered. The villagers of Cattistock did later recall that Widow Whistle had been rather flush with money after her husband died, but had just assumed he had left her a tidy sum.

As for the unfortunate victim's name, well, Widow Whistle had never asked him and had never cared. But the locals were in no doubt. It was Wat Perkins. And after the reunited head and body were given a decent Christian burial the ghost walked no more. Presumably its task was done.

## BEAMINSTER

Colonel Broadrepp of Mapperton Manor was the Justice of the Peace for the area around Beaminster in the early 18th century, and he took his job seriously. In 1728 he was faced with a situation that would have daunted many men, but Colonel Broadrepp was equal to the task.

John Daniel, a 14-year-old boy, had died in the last week of May 1728, his body being found in a field on his father's farm. The boy's stepmother, Elizabeth Daniel, told the coroner that the boy had periodically suffered from violent fits. This was accepted as the cause of death and the poor boy was buried.

A month later Colonel Broadrepp was contacted by the parents of Hannah Daniel, John's mother, a good lady who had died in childbirth fourteen years earlier. They said that they wanted to exhume the body of their grandson John. Foul play in the death of the boy was suspected. When the Colonel asked why they had not voiced their concerns before the funeral, the old folk replied that they had not had any suspicions then, only now more than a month later. And it was the haunting that had made them change their minds.

---

*The church at Beaminster which was the venue for one of the best attested and most carefully investigated spectral apparitions of Dorset's paranormal history.*

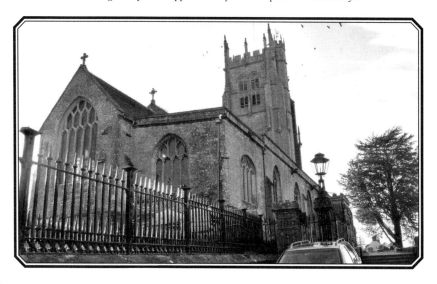

*The spectral woman of Beaminster is dressed in country clothes of the 18th century, which help to identify her.*

On 27th June, twelve schoolboys had been playing in the churchyard. The boys heard the sounds of singing, although the church was empty, but do not seem to have been unduly worried by the manifestation. A few minutes later one boy went into the church to collect his books before going home, the gallery of the church doubling up as their schoolroom. The boy was startled to see a white coffin in the gallery, though there had not been one there earlier and nobody had entered the church. The boy ran off to call his companions and together the twelve boys returned.

They found the strange coffin still there, with a ribbon tied around one handle. It had now been joined by the apparition of a teenage boy who was sitting at a desk with a pen in his hand as if doing some schoolwork. Around his hand was wrapped a white cloth. 'There sits our John,' piped up the dead boy's half brother, Isaac, 'with a coat on such as I have and with a pen in his hand.' The boy snatched up a stone and threw it at the apparition, which promptly vanished.

Colonel Broadrepp sent for the boys and quizzed them. He paid particular attention to the testimony of a boy who was new to Beaminster and had not known John Daniel in life. Broadrepp then sent for the couple who had prepared the body for burial to ask if they had noticed anything unusual. The woman recalled that the boy's right hand had been bandaged to cover a cut that appeared to be a few days old. The man remarked that he had thought it strange that Elizabeth Daniel had already got the boy's body into its shroud as this was a job usually left to him and his wife.

Agreeing that something was odd, Broadrepp ordered the body to be exhumed. The shroud was pulled back and there, around the boy's neck, was a clear black line. He had been strangled with a piece of string or thin rope. Suspicion at once centred on Elizabeth Daniel. It was she who had put forward the story about fits and who had prepared the shroud. Perhaps she wanted the Daniel lands to go to her own son, rather than to John, or perhaps she had simply lost her temper with her stepson one day. There was, however, no real evidence against her so she escaped trial. She did not escape the condemnation of her neighbours, however, for all the locals believed that she had caused the boy's death.

Strangely, it was not the ghost of John Daniel that continued to be seen in and around the church at Beaminster in the years after 1728, but that of his mother Hannah. She is seen still from time to time. Wearing a dark-coloured dress that falls to her ankles, with a brightly coloured floral print scarf wrapped over her shoulders, the ghost wears a wide-brimmed straw bonnet. She has a pale face and those who see her report that she seems to be looking for something – or perhaps for someone.

## STOKE ABBOTT

The little village of Stoke Abbott lies a mile or so south-west of Beaminster along a narrow, winding lane that climbs steeply in places. The village is, today, dominated by watering holes of two distinct kinds. The first is a natural spring that pours tumbling waters into a stone basin, which has a metal cup chained to it for use by passers-by. The other is a welcoming pub that offers meals, ales and hospitality to those for whom spring water is not enough.

The ghost of Stoke Abbott dates back many years, though both spring and pub were already present in those days. The phantom in question is known only as The Old Squire, nobody seems to know either his name or the date when he lived. He was, by all accounts, a fearsome man with a savage temper. Even after his death, The Old Squire is not a man to cross. He drives his coach and four from Stoke Abbott over the hill towards Beaminster with the same furious energy with which he lived his life. Whipping the horses to a gallop of terrifying speed, the Old

Squire races along the narrow lanes, threatening to run over any that he meets on the way.

Fortunately the phantom coach always manages to disappear before a collision with an approaching car or pedestrian, though it remains a startling sight.

# BROADWINDSOR

The B3162 running west from Broadwindsor to Drimpton is not particularly remarkable at first sight. Nor, indeed, at second sight. It is, however, the venue for a quite remarkable haunting.

Led by a black hearse drawn by four black horses, each adorned with a black ostrich feather plume, a funeral cortege makes its way down the hill into Broadwindsor. Those who have seen the apparition tend to think that it is a perfectly normal funeral, though a horse-drawn hearse is unusual these days. They report that there seems to be quite a crowd following the coffin and presume it to be some grand affair of the present day, until, that is, the entire cavalcade vanishes into thin air. Witnessing this can be quite an alarming experience.

*The church at Broadwindsor is the destination for a phantom funeral that proceeds along the B3162, but never reaches the churchyard.*

The procession has been seen at various times at various places along the road, always moving slowly toward Broadwindsor. Strangely, the phantom funeral has never been seen to arrive at the church itself.

# BETTISCOMBE

The screaming skull of Bettiscombe is probably the best known haunting of Dorset, certainly outside the county. And yet all is not what it may appear.

According to the generally accepted legend of the screaming skull, the story began in 1685 when James, Duke of Monmouth, landed in Dorset to raise a Protestant rebellion against his Catholic uncle, King James II. Azariah Pinney, son of John Pinney who owned Bettiscombe, joined the Monmouth Rising. The rebellion ended in defeat and young Azariah, along with hundreds of others, was dragged before a court and charged with treason. Found guilty, Azariah was sentenced to death, though the authorities ruled that his life would be spared if the sum of £65 could be found. Azariah's sister Hester put up the money, so, instead of being hanged, the young man was shipped as a slave to the West Indies.

Azariah later won his freedom and rose to be a prominent merchant on the island of Nevis. In 1705 John Pinney died and his son came home to take over the family estates. Azariah brought with him a faithful black companion, a man who had once been a fellow slave on the sugar plantations of Nevis. As the first black man to be seen in that part of Dorset, he made a great impression on the local folk.

When he died, Azariah's friend was buried in Bettiscombe church, but he did not rest in peace. Bettiscombe House was plagued by terrifying screams, slamming doors and crashing furniture. Only then did Azariah recall that he and his companion had sworn never to be separated. The body was dug up and, although only a few days had passed, the skull was found to be entirely clean of flesh of any kind. The gleaming, grinning skull was taken from the grave and carried to Bettiscombe House where it was put high up in the roof timbers.

There it rested until the middle of the 19th century. Bettiscombe House was then being rented out as a farm and the new tenant did not much fancy his grim companion. He took down the skull and threw it

*The manor of Bettiscombe harbours perhaps the most famous phantom of Dorset, though all is not what it seems in this picturesque hamlet. The manor is a working farm.*

into the nearby pond. At once the house was plagued by disturbances. Screams once more echoed through the rooms and doors were slammed shut by unseen hands. After less than a week, the farmer headed for the pond armed with a hay rake with which he combed the waters until he retrieved the skull. It has not left the house since.

In 1963 a professor of anatomy inspected the skull and declared it to be that of a European woman aged about 30. So much for the legend of a faithful black companion. It has been suggested that the skull may have come from one of the prehistoric barrows that dot the hills around Bettiscombe. Antiquarians of the 17th century were known to have dug open such tombs and taken the contents as souvenirs.

According to Michael Pinney, a descendant of Azariah, the whole story was concocted in the 1830s by another ancestor, Anna Maria Pinney. This was the time when gothic horror stories, such as *Frankenstein*, were hugely popular. Following the genre, young Anna took some genuine local tales and wove them together into the legend of the screaming skull. The story of Azariah and his escapades was true enough and the skull was a very real presence in the house – said to be a good luck charm. There was also a ghostly presence in the attic which took the form of heavy footsteps pacing back and forth. Imagination, it would seem, did the rest.

Whatever its origins may be, the skull of Bettiscombe retains a powerful aura. It is perhaps wise to leave it where it is.

Also best left alone is the Wishing Stone, an ancient megalith that stands proud and alone on the hillside high above Bettiscombe. As its name suggests, this standing stone has the power to grant wishes, but Midsummer's Night is not the time to come here in search of help. On that shortest night of the year the stone tears itself free of the ground and lumbers down the hill to drink at the small stream in the valley below. Then, as dawn approaches, it climbs back up to its ancient home.

Also on the move is the phantom hearse that haunts the lane outside Bettiscombe church. Whose funeral is being recreated, or what the apparition might mean, nobody is terribly certain but, drawn by a pair of black horses, the black carriage moves slowly towards the church in total silence.

# LYME REGIS

The town of Lyme Regis leapt temporarily to national fame in 1685 when the Duke of Monmouth landed here to raise his doomed rebellion against his tyrannical uncle, King James II. Although the uprising would end in disaster, it began well enough. Monmouth was popular, young and handsome so the good citizens of Lyme Regis cheered him loudly when he came ashore. Monmouth happily acknowledged the encouragement and rode inland to raise what he hoped would be a successful army of rebels. It is those happy days that the ghostly Monmouth returns to Lyme Regis to recreate. Mounted on

*The famous Cobb breakwater protects the harbour of Lyme Regis where the ill-fated Duke of Monmouth landed to begin his rebellion in 1685.*

a white charger and waving jovially to an invisible crowd of well-wishers, the young Duke rides inland from the harbour.

The disastrous end of the Monmouth uprising has also left its spectral mark in Lyme Regis. After crushing the rebellion, King James II sent his chief judge, George Jeffreys, to mete out savage justice to the rebels. He opened his court in Lyme Regis on 11 September 1685 and before sunset had sentenced twelve local men to hang. One of those unfortunates haunts Broad Street, down which he was led to be hanged on a gibbet erected on the famous harbour breakwater known as The Cobb. The ghostly man staggers down the hill with his head lolling gruesomely from side to side.

Judge Jeffreys himself is said to haunt the house where he stayed while in Lyme Regis. This Great House, as it was known, is now Boots the Chemist. The upper floors are today occupied by offices so there is nobody there at night to see if the phantom Jeffreys still wanders the corridors carrying a bloodstained rag in his hand.

# CHARMOUTH

The White Lady of Charmouth is one of the more active and best attested ghosts in Dorset. She lurks along The Street, the old main road that climbs up out of the village to the east, heading towards Bridport, where she has been seen by dozens of motorists.

Whenever she appears, the ghost behaves in much the same way. She runs along the side of the road as if trying to get away from someone – or something. She wears a long dress of pale or white material that flaps about as she runs, almost as if she is racing into a wind. She will then dart across the road and vanish from sight as she races off down to the River Char. Time was the local press took an interest in the White Lady of Charmouth but, as so often happens with ghosts, there was no explanation to be had and no real story to follow up. She is seen as much now as she ever was, but reports seldom tend to make the press.

Strangely, there is a second ghost along the same stretch of road. This is of a man dressed in a long coat, or cloak, of dark brown colour. For some reason, this phantom is generally said to be a monk though there is no record of any monastery ever having stood here. He may just as

*This milestone stands beside the road near where the White Lady of Charmouth is often reported appearing. Some suspect that the milestone, seen in misty conditions, might be mistaken for the ghost.*

easily be a secular man dressed in a dark coat. He could be linked to the White Lady, of course, and might be the cause of her obvious terror. But if and how they are linked is quite unknown.

Also unknown are the origins of the lights and flames seen to shoot up into the sky along cliffs near Charmouth. Reported most often by sailors and yachtsmen coasting in the late evening, the lights appear to move along the most inaccessible cliffs and precipitous slopes. They are generally reckoned to be paranormal in origin and have been termed the ghost lights of Charmouth.

# CHIDEOCK

The lane running down into Chideock from the north appears ordinary enough, but it is not a place to linger after dark. This is a route patrolled by a monstrous black hound, an apparition that appears in several places around Dorset.

This particular black dog is in the habit of following people as they walk along the lane, which must be most unnerving, but it also likes to lope around the churchyard or sit patiently beside a tomb as if waiting for someone. The hound is described as being much larger than any mortal dog and covered in long, shaggy fur. The most disturbing aspect of the dog is its blazing red eyes that seem to have some inner fire. These sort of dogs are generally held to bring bad luck in their wake, though the hound of Chideock has no such stories attached to it.

The origin of these black dogs, that are found all across England, is somewhat obscure. Some local legends link them to the Devil, holding that they are hell hounds sent out to patrol the world to search for the souls of the damned or to foment evil at the bidding of their master. However, some believe that these legends merely mask the fact that the dogs were linked to the old pagan religion and were subsequently demonised by the new religion of Christianity. They are often associated with ancient earthworks or standing stones or, as at Chideock, with holy places where a Christian church is thought to have been built over a pagan site.

Whatever their origins or their purpose, it is probably best to leave well alone. Anyone who sees the great black dog padding silently down the lane to Chideock church would do well to look the other way and pass on quickly.

A second ghost haunts the same lane. This is the phantom of a Catholic priest who lived in Chideock in the early 19th century. The local gentry had been Catholic throughout the long centuries when to practise the religion openly was to court unpopularity or even prosecution. A small Catholic chapel was maintained at North Chideock and it was the priest who ministered here whose ghost is seen. According to local stories he fell in love with the young widow who lived in Clock House, which stands opposite the Church of England

---

*Chideock's phantom priest walks disconsolately down this lane, as he did so often in life.*

*The pub car park in Chideock where a phantom lady was seen very clearly a few years ago. She was standing at a spot just to the right of the parked car in the picture.*

church in the centre of the village. Torn between his faith and his love, the unfortunate man would wander often down the lane to chat to his beloved, who had no idea of his feelings. Time came when the woman married and the priest confessed everything to his bishop. He was sent to a distant ministry where, it was hoped, he would find peace. Presumably he did not, for his ghost walks to this day, following the route he walked so often in life.

The Clock House is today a charming and welcoming pub and it has its own ghost. Interestingly, it is of a young woman in a smock or loose gown. She is seen infrequently, but with startling clarity. In the 1990s the then landlord drove home one summer's evening with his wife from a social event. He pulled into the car park with no thought other than to wonder how his barman had been coping without him. Standing right in the centre of the car park was the young lady in the loose dress. She turned to look at the approaching publican, smiled gently and then vanished abruptly. The landlord turned to his wife to ask if she had seen the ghost. 'Yes,' came the reply, 'she had no legs. Wasn't that odd?'

# BRIDPORT

The town of Bridport made its fortune from rope. The broad pavements of the high street were formerly festooned with ropes, nets, strings and a whole host of similar products being twisted, woven, tied and dried. When sailing ships relied on good rope for virtually everything, Bridport was of key strategic importance to both commerce and the fighting navy.

It was this busy, vibrant and prosperous town that drew Squire Light of Baglake House to visit in January 1748. Squire Light was a well known local rake. There was no malice in the man, but there was usually rather too much wine for his own good. Chasing women, starting fights and generally making a nuisance of himself were the chief delights of Squire Light, alongside hunting and racing horses.

Quite what it was that brought Squire Light into Bridport on 12th January we shall never know. He said he had to see a man on business, but did not reveal who the mysterious businessman was. He came back late in the afternoon in a foul temper. After moodily walking about the house and shouting at the servants for an hour or more, Squire Light called for his horse to be saddled and rode off. Fearing something was wrong, his groom saddled a second horse and set off in pursuit. He was too late. Squire Light had reached the River Mangerton and drowned himself.

The groom dragged the body out of the river and set off to report the suicide. As he trotted sadly homeward, he was startled to meet the phantom of his master riding towards the river. The groom fell from his horse and never really recovered from the shock, remaining jumpy and nervous for the rest of his days.

The ghostly shade of Squire Light may still be seen riding down to the banks of the River Mangerton. There he springs down from his horse and vanishes. Whoever he met in Bridport that fatal day and whatever they discussed, the repercussions are still to be seen.

Perhaps rather more disturbing is the grey lady of Gipsy Lane, a little thoroughfare off Pymore Road. This ghost is seen more often by children

*Bridport's town museum has bravely acquired a haunted dress to add to its wide range of exhibits. The garment will feel at home as there are already at least two ghosts in the ancient building.*

than by adults. She wears a grey dress, carries a grey rolled up umbrella, has grey hair and even her face has the grey pallor of death about it. Although she invariably smiles, there is nothing pleasant about this spectre. Her smile is one of cunning malevolence, and few who see her are in any doubt that she is intent on evil. Sometimes the ghost just stands and watches, but at other times she will beckon to children or hold out her arms as if reaching toward the youngsters. She is best avoided.

Considerably more welcoming is the genial old gent who haunts what is now Bridport Museum in South Street. The building is more than four centuries old, having been built as a coaching inn but later doing service as a bank, a club and a private house. It is the owner of the building from Edwardian times, one Captain Albert Codd, who haunts the place. He is seen dressed in what was his favourite smoking jacket of bright yellow hue and black trousers. Captain Codd loved his house, and left it to the town council to serve as a museum. He is presumably happy with the results for his ghost seems to be most at ease and relaxed. In January 2006 he appeared to a member of staff. The old boy smiled gently, then turned and walked around a corner to vanish completely.

The museum may also have a haunted fireplace. The chimney from the grand fireplace in the main room on the ground floor is blocked off and no fire is ever lit there, the building having efficient central heating.

Despite this, visitors sometimes see a fire blazing merrily in the grate and a young lady in Victorian costume warming herself by the flames.

In 2005 the museum acquired a new and rather sinister exhibit in the form of a haunted dress. The beautiful 17th-century gown was left to the museum and is undoubtedly a fine example of the work of local seamstresses. However, it also attracts a young lady ghost who walks about the vicinity of wherever the dress is at the time. She seems to be rather protective of the garment, as if it holds some special memories for her. She is no real bother, except for the fact that she appears with startling regularity. No wonder the dress was bequeathed to the museum.

*The sign of the much haunted Bull Hotel in Bridport gives no hint of the spectres that lurk within.*

More active still are the ghosts of the Bull Hotel in East Street. The ancient pub is thought to have been built over a small medieval graveyard, which may account for the disembodied voices that are heard here quite frequently – especially in the toilets for some reason. More specifically, the pub is haunted by the ghost of Wadham Strangeways who was killed here in bizarre fashion in 1685.

In June that year the Duke of Monmouth landed at Lyme Regis with a force of 82 men to claim the throne from his uncle, King James II. One of Monmouth's first moves was to send men galloping in all directions to raise recruits and to seek news of the royal army. At Bridport, Monmouth's scouts were met with hostility and gunshots. In the skirmish that followed, the unfortunate Wadham Strangeways, a resident of Bridport, took refuge in the Bull Hotel. A bullet fired by the skirmishers outside came through the window and struck Strangeways.

He was carried to a table at the foot of the stairs, where he passed away. It is often said that his ghost ceased to appear after the fatal window was blocked up, but the blocked window is in a newer part of the building. In any case, his ghost walks still.

Rather less trouble is the phantom lady who appears in the reception area of the hotel. She is dressed in a country suit that looks rather old fashioned but not at all out of place in Bridport as the 21st century begins. The middle-aged lady sits in a chair nestled into a corner and chats away animatedly to an invisible companion. In 2006 one member of staff reported that the tweedy ghost appears often: 'She is here once or twice a month. Just sits there chatting away for a minute or two, then suddenly she is gone. She's quite friendly. Obviously a kind soul.'

## Loders

The Yellow Lane in the village of Loders has an unhappy reputation. Some time in the 19th century a coachman was urged to make the best time possible home from Bridport. Knowing that a fine reward awaited him for a quick journey, the man chose to take a short cut up Yellow Lane, although it was not a main road and was usually frequented only by pedestrians and shepherds.

The lane points straight toward the distant Eggardon Hill, which is a known

*The haunted Yellow Lane of Loders takes its name from the yellow sandstone through which it has been cut.*

haunt of the Devil and a rendezvous for other unworldly creatures. Perhaps the driver was distracted by something. We will never know, but certainly he did not see the low branch that projected dangerously across the road. The branch caught him in the face, tearing his head from his shoulders.

The ghostly echoes of that hideous accident remain to this day. The horrific figure of a man lacking his head is seen from time to time staggering down Yellow Lane.

# EGGARDON HILL

The wind-blasted heights of Eggardon Hill are not a place to linger. The wind howls in off the English Channel and this towering hill is the first high point it reaches. Even when the air is still and calm in the valleys below, the treeless slopes above are whipped by the wind. In winter this is a bleak and lonely spot, in summer exposed and sombre.

*The mysterious heights of Eggardon Hill dominate the skyline for miles around.*

Eggardon Hill is one of the most impressive heights in Dorset. It rears up over 800 feet above sea level. The crest of the hill is dominated by powerful earthwork fortifications that in pre-Roman times protected a prosperous Celtic settlement. Around the slopes of the hill are dotted burial mounds and field works from even earlier eras. This is a place steeped in history.

It may be steeped in much else besides for this is a strange place. There is said to be a phantom white deer that lives on the hill and which brings bad luck to all who see her, while disembodied screams have the power to shock all who hear them. In the days when horses provided the motive power for carts and carriages, the hill was notorious for the fact that horses would unaccountably refuse to pass over it. Although the driver could see nothing, the horse most certainly could and would refuse to budge. Dogs were also liable to turn tail and flee when asked to go up Eggardon Hill.

These days most people prefer the internal combustion engine to horses, but the hill has not lost its power to cause problems. Several motorists have reported that their engines have cut out quite suddenly, only to start again without difficulty a few minutes later. One person who suffered this in 2005 reported: 'I was driving along happy as Larry, when the car just cut out. That is a narrow road up there and there was no passing space close enough, so I just coasted to a stop. Of course, I knew the stories about the Devil and such and did not believe a word of it. But I tell you this. Being stuck up on Eggardon Hill all alone with the dusk closing down and not a living soul in sight is a spooky experience. Suddenly the stories did not seem so silly. Fortunately the car started up again when I fired the ignition. I drove off pretty smartly, I can tell you.'

All this bother may be related to the very solid apparitions that are sometimes seen wandering around the slopes of this hill. These phantom creatures come in the form of gigantic black dogs with glowing eyes and long shaggy hair. These monstrous dogs are, as elsewhere, said to be the hounds of the Devil. But, at Eggardon Hill, the Evil One himself comes out to put his pack on the trail of their quarry. On stormy nights, it is said, the Devil will sit on top of Eggardon Hill scanning the Dorset countryside for those who have been evil enough to deserve a place in Hell. When he spies them, the Devil lets loose his pack of demonic dogs to race over the countryside and hunt down the souls of the damned.

This might be dismissed as merely an old story were it not for the strange events that are reported to swirl around the hilltop. And for the fact that in the 1950s a man out walking his own dog met a tall, dark haired man apparently exercising two large black hounds. For some reason suddenly nervous, the dog walker hurried back to his car. As he glanced over his shoulder he saw the stranger and his dogs set off at a run, and thought he saw sparks flying from the man's boots as they struck the ground.

And it may be entirely coincidental that Eggardon Hill is the place in Dorset where UFOs and flying saucers are seen more often than anywhere else.

It is a strange place indeed.

## KINGSTON RUSSELL

The elegant mansion of Kingston Russell takes its name from the Russell family, which acquired these lands in the 14th century and, in the reign of King Henry VIII, built an impressive manor house here. The family later won the title of Duke of Bedford and moved to Woburn Abbey. The manor at Kingston Russell was rebuilt in the 17th century and then, in 1730, was clad in the current elegant Georgian façade.

The house and grounds are not open to the public, but the spectacular ghostly vision associated with Kingston Russell is as visible in the lanes to the south as it is at the house itself. The manifestation takes the form of a Death Coach, a terrifying apparition peculiar to the south-western counties of England. This awful vision has been seen rattling down the slope from Ashley Chase to the south. The hill is crowned by a

The drive leading to Kingston Russell House is the route taken by the infamous Death Coach, though its mission is not clear.

prehistoric stone circle, a long barrow and a host of round barrows, indicating that its links to the spirit world are ancient indeed.

The Death Coach is driven by a headless coachman, while an equally headless footman stands on the pillion behind. The terrible vehicle comes down the hill, turns into the gates of Kingston Russell House and clatters up to the front door. The coach halts there for a while as if waiting for somebody to come out and climb aboard. After a few minutes the coachman whips his horses into a trot. They pull the coach back up the drive, turning left to return up the hill to the ancient monuments that crown the summit.

Who it is that the Death Coach comes to collect is not clear. The only person of any fame to have a close connection to the present house was Sir Thomas Masterman Hardy, the naval captain who cradled Lord Nelson as he lay dying at the Battle of Trafalgar in 1805. Hardy is generally regarded as having been a talented and humane sea captain who rose to the ranks of First Sea Lord and Governor of Greenwich Hospital, so it seems unlikely that the doom-laden vehicle is for him. Perhaps it calls for some past resident of the house who managed to keep his sins secret – at least from mortals, if not from the driver of the Death Coach.

# BINCOMBE

The hills above Bincombe are dotted with ancient burial barrows, some of which date back to the Bronze Age more than 3,000 years ago. These rounded earthen mounds were built to house the remains of warriors, chieftains and priests. Buried with their treasures and weapons, the dead have rested for millennia beneath the green turf of Dorset.

*The rail tunnel at Bincombe is haunted by a mysterious ghostly pedestrian.*

Such barrows can be found right across Dorset, but those on the hills above Bincombe are haunted in dramatic and surprising fashion. At noon on summer's days the barrows echo to the sound of singing. It is a very gentle singing and remarkably pleasant, and it seems to come from somewhere deep beneath the ground.

Very different is the phenomenon which appears here on winter nights. Then the barrows will, on occasion, pour forth a column of flame that shoots upward with an orange intensity that tears open the night sky. The fiery pillar burns brightly for a few seconds, then vanishes as abruptly as it appeared, leaving behind no trace of scorching or ash on the turf.

Just to the west of the barrows the mainline railway from London to Weymouth cuts through the hills by way of a tunnel. It is the tunnel that is haunted by a man who walks with stumbling tread and bowed head. More than one train driver has thought he has run down some hapless member of the public, only to find no sign of a body nor of anything that might have looked like a person. In 1991 a driver went so far as to call the police, but even the most dedicated search by the local constabulary could find nothing.

Could this be the ghost of some unfortunate who was, indeed, run down by a train in Bincombe Tunnel?

## WEYMOUTH

The mouth of the River Wey has been a favoured anchorage for generations. The Romans tied up their merchant ships here, as did the Saxons. The town of Weymouth sent 20 ships to help King Edward III attack France in the 14th century and sent six armed with cannon to face the Spanish Armada of 1588.

However, it was the growing naval importance of nearby Portland that led the British government to fortify the approaches with Nothe Fort in mid-Victorian times. The precautions were prompted by the

*Nothe Fort was completed in 1872, but the ghost only dates back to the 1940s.*

threat of hostilities with France and the construction was intended to mount twelve of the new rifled heavy cannon then entering service.

The Fort was completed in 1872, together with other defensive works around the town, and the army moved in to take up occupation. Later, the original guns were replaced with fewer, but more powerful weapons, just in time for the First World War. These were fired in anger only once and that was during the Second World War, in July 1940 when a pair of ships was spotted approaching without lights. The guns fired warning shots, when the two ships at once switched on their lights to reveal that they were packed with refugees fleeing the German invaders of the Channel Islands.

It was, however, at about this time that the ghost first began to be seen. Nothe Fort was largely given over to anti-aircraft guns and ammunition storage during the Second World War, so the old gun batteries were deserted unless action beckoned. Sentries began reporting seeing a man walking these lonely walls, but there was never anyone there when the guard was turned out to check. The figure seems an enigmatic one. By rights it should be a soldier of some date, but no details of a uniform are ever noted. He manifests as a shadowy figure who slips in and out of view without ever appearing with any clarity.

To enter into the spirit of things, the Weymouth Civic Society, which now runs the fort as a tourist attraction, has installed an electronic 'ghost'. This figure leaps about and stares with evil-glowing eyes when set off by a passing tourist. The Society has recently won a grant from the Lottery Fund to undertake a £2.4 million restoration of the Fort. It remains to be seen if the real ghost continues to haunt the place when the work is done.

# ISLE OF PORTLAND

The Isle of Portland is, in fact, linked to the mainland by the great sweeping shingle strand of Chesil Bank – one of the natural wonders of the world – and by a modern causeway carrying the A354. Until the 19th century, however, this area was a remote and strange place populated by a few shepherds and fishermen in scattered villages. Then, in 1849, the Royal Navy began the construction of the massive naval base of Portland Harbour which has dominated the place ever since.

The change of emphasis has done nothing to put off the ancient ghosts. The most notorious is the Tow Dog, another of the gigantic black hounds that haunt so much of Dorset. This particular dog is best treated with caution, but does not seem to be directly linked to the Devil. He behaves in an odd fashion for a phantom black dog, preferring to stand resolutely in the path of pedestrians or oncoming cars and forcing them to stop. As soon as he has gained the undivided attention he seems to crave, the Tow Dog vanishes.

# • East Dorset •

## CHETTLE

On 16th December 1780 a notoriously violent, ruthless and successful gang of poachers reached the end of their criminal career. And the ghostly echoes of the event still haunt Chettle. The leader of the poachers was known to be Trumpet Major Blandford of the dragoons, but nobody was willing to testify against him. If he were to be brought to justice he would have to be caught red-handed, so the gamekeepers of Cranborne Chase decided to do just that.

Hearing through an informant that Blandford would be after deer on the fateful night of 16th December, together with six companions, the keepers mustered in strength armed with pistols, swords and clubs. Soon after midnight they sprang their ambush at a gateway up on Chettle Common where five paths met. The poachers were likewise armed and fought back. The savage moonlit struggle came to an end only when Blandford fell to the ground with his left arm severed below the elbow.

Blandford was carried away to a nearby hunting lodge where a tourniquet was put around his arm, and his fellows were trussed up and put under arrest. Blandford was handed over to the civil authorities and a trial was arranged in Dorchester: he was sent to prison for seven years. Upon his release Blandford found that his lost hand and lower arm had been buried in Pimperne churchyard and the site of the fight had become famous as Bloody Shard Gate. He moved to London where he set himself up as a game merchant, prospering at his shop near Lincoln's Inn Fields as late as 1818.

Blandford died soon after, which is when the hauntings began. Walking with head down-turned as if searching for something, the phantom figure of a man began to be seen blundering about at Bloody Shard Gate. If the identity of the ghost were in any doubt, it was removed by the fact that the spectre's left arm was missing below the elbow. The ghost of Bloody Shard Gate is seen surprisingly often. The five paths still meet here and all are popular with walkers taking advantage of the scenery of Cranborne Chase. It is they who report the ghost most often these days.

It was a crime of a very different kind that led to the haunting of Eastbury House, to the west of Chettle. The house is impressive enough, but is a mere shadow of the vast mansion erected here by George Bubb in 1720. Bubb had inherited the estate and a large sum of money from a cousin he had barely known and he was soon showing all who knew him that he intended to enjoy his good fortune to the limit. As well as the drinking, carousing and womanising that might have been expected, Bubb hired the famous architect Sir John Vanbrugh to build him a new mansion at Eastbury. Bubb entered Society in London, becoming a Member of Parliament and noted man about town.

Down in Dorset, however, all was not well. Bubb had hired an estate manager by the name of William Doggett to care for the country estates that were the main source of his wealth. Unfortunately, Doggett was as dishonest as he was talented and for years he filched sums of impressive size from his employer, while managing to hide his crimes in the complexities of bookkeeping.

It could not last, of course. In the later 1740s Bubb became concerned by his disappearing wealth. Still not suspecting Doggett, Bubb sent him a message saying that he would be arriving at Eastbury in a day or two so that the two men could go through the books together and track down what had gone wrong.

Realising that he was to be found out, Doggett shot himself. Bubb was appalled, as much by the disloyalty of a man he had trusted as by the vast sums that were found to be missing. Lands had to be sold and mortgages incurred – the estates were never the same again. The upkeep of the mighty house, built by Vanbrugh, could not be afforded so much of it was demolished.

Doggett's crimes obviously weighed heavy on his conscience. A few weeks after his suicide, the ghost of Doggett returned to Eastbury. He was seen walking slowly down the long drive from the house to the lane that leads to the village of Tarrant Gunville. There the spectre stood waiting patiently for a few minutes until a coach drawn by four black horses pulled up. Once Doggett was inside, the coachman burst out into maniacal laughter and whipped the horses into gallop.

Those few villagers who saw this frightful apparition were convinced that they had seen the Devil himself arrive in his Death Coach to collect the damned soul of the wicked Doggett. If so, the Devil certainly enjoyed his visit for the ghostly scene has been played out several times since. Sometimes it is merely the ghost of Doggett who is seen waiting beside the gates of Eastbury House, but the Devil still comes calling now and again.

## BOTTLEBUSH DOWN

That the windswept, grassy slopes of Bottlebush Down were haunted by a ghostly horseman was a well known fact in the area. Two teenage girls cycling home to Handley from a dance even reported him to the police – though as a stalker who had followed them for some distance in aggressive mood. The haunting could have remained one of those mysterious ghostly apparitions, of which Dorset has so many, were it not for Dr Richard Chaloner Clay.

Dr Clay was a leading archaeologist who was drawn to Bottlebush Down by the large number of prehistoric remains to be found there. A Roman road, now a bridleway, was cut arrow straight over the hills to replace an older, more winding prehistoric track. Alongside this track the Bronze Age inhabitants of Dorset had carved a mighty cursus, an oval-shaped earthwork comprising a ditch and bank, some 12 feet tall and four miles long. There are also dozens of burial mounds of all shapes and sizes, plus a variety of more domestic remains.

One evening Dr Clay was in his car driving home across Bottlebush

*The ancient burial barrow on Bottlebush Down that is the home for what may be the oldest ghost in all England.*

Down when he saw a rider about 100 yards away across the downs. At first Dr Clay thought the rider was from the nearby racing stables, but then something happened to make him change his mind.

'Suddenly he turned his horse's head and galloped as if to reach the road ahead before my car arrived there. I was so interested that I changed gear to slow my car's speed in order that we should meet and I should be able to find out why he had taken this sudden action. Before I had drawn level with him, he turned his horse again to the north and galloped along parallel to me about 50 yards from the road. I could now see that he was no ordinary horseman, for he had bare legs and wore a long, loose coat. The horse had a long mane and tail, but I could see no bridle or stirrups. The rider's face was turned towards me, but I could not see his features. He seemed to be threatening me with some implement which he waved in his right hand above his head. I tried hard to identify the weapon, for I suddenly realised that he was a prehistoric man, but I failed. It seemed to be on a 2 ft shaft. After travelling parallel to my car for about 100 yards, the rider and horse suddenly vanished. I noted the spot and next day found at the spot a low round barrow.'

Dr Clay's specialist knowledge and close encounter with the horseman allowed him to date the rider to the later Bronze Age, which transpired to be the same date as the barrow by which the apparition had vanished. It seems likely that the spectral horseman is the ghost of the long-dead warrior whose mortal remains lie buried beneath the round barrow. This would make him the oldest phantom in Dorset, and possibly in all England.

*The mounted warrior of Bottlebush Down carries weapons and equipment that date him back to the Bronze Age.*

## GUSSAGE ALL SAINTS

Anthony Ashley Cooper was the type of man who gives politicians a bad name. He was undoubtedly charming, clever and hardworking, but he was also notoriously devious, dishonest and untrustworthy. It is heart-warming to know that he was eventually found out and punished for his crimes.

Cooper first came to notice when he left his native Dorset to join the Royalist army on the outbreak of the English Civil War in 1642. Two years later, Cooper saw the way things were going, so he abandoned the King and joined the forces of Parliament. So talented was he that he rose to become a member of Oliver Cromwell's Council of State. Cooper prospered, betraying the secrets of his former friends and using his talents to reform the business of state. In 1660 Cooper once more changed sides, dumping his enthusiasm for Parliamentary rule and being the first member of the Council of State to cross the sea to France and pledge loyalty to the exiled King Charles II, who was back on his throne later that year.

Charles made Cooper the Chancellor of the Exchequer and raised him to the peerage as Earl of Shaftesbury. Shaftesbury, as he now was, intrigued his way around government, getting rivals sacked for no good reason and promoting his favourites. He over reached himself when he tried to get the Duke of York, and future King James II, cut out of the succession. Shaftesbury joined forces with Titus Oates in publicising an entirely fictitious plot by the Catholic Church to murder King Charles II and put the Catholic Duke of York on the throne instead. In the furore that followed 35 men were executed for supposed treason, but finally the machinations of Oates and Shaftesbury were uncovered. Shaftesbury was tried for treason and, although he was acquitted, King Charles sent him into exile where he died in 1683.

It is this rather unpleasant character who haunts the lanes around Gussage All Saints. Riding in his coach, the Earl of Shaftesbury trots around the area where he once lived and owned much land. It is said that he will sometimes stop and invite passers-by to climb up into his phantom coach. To date nobody has been brave enough to accept the invitation – or if they have, they have not survived to tell the tale.

# KNOWLTON

The ruined church of Knowlton stands in the middle of an ancient henge that dates back at least 4,000 years to the Neolithic Age, before the knowledge of how to make metal tools had reached Britain. The site has been considered sacred for longer than perhaps any other in England.

The ghosts that lurk here seem to date back to pagan days. The tall man dressed in a long cloak who walks about the inner ring of the earthen bank that marks the outside of the henge is generally held to be a pagan priest of some kind, while the great black hound that patrols outside is marked down as a dog of the Devil – but then Christianity viewed all the old gods as devils. Certainly local people believe that it is the henge alone that keeps the ghosts trapped inside and protects the surrounding Christians from pagan wrath.

*At Knowlton a prehistoric henge surrounds a medieval Christian church. The ghost is thought to belong to the older, pagan construction.*

The medieval church is ruined, as it has been for many years. In its time the church was famous for having a magnificent peal of three bells. When the church was closed, one bell was taken to Sturminster Marshall and a second to Shapwick, but the largest and finest was left at Knowlton. In the mid 19th century a gang of crooks decided to steal it, take it to France and sell it. They got the bell only so far as Sturminster Newton. The horse pulling the cart on which the bell was loaded refused to cross the Stour. No amount of whipping would persuade the horse to move, but in the commotion the cart overturned and the bell fell into the river.

The local folk rallied to the cause and next day came with horses and ropes to pull the bell out of the river so that it could be restored to its proper place. Again the horses refused to work. And when the men tried brute human muscle power, the ropes broke. And so the bell remained in the Stour where, when flood waters rage down the stream, it can be heard tolling as it tumbles about.

# BLANDFORD

The handsome Georgian town of Blandford gained its present elegant face from the massive rebuilding that followed the disastrous fire of 1731, which burned so hot that the church bells melted. The town has long been famous for its army base, at which the Duke of Wellington once served. And the base has long been the focus for rumours of hauntings.

In 1952 three young men doing national service were hauled up before their regimental commander on a charge of fighting in barracks. The men explained the night-time fracas by stating that they had not been fighting, but trying to barricade the door against a ghost. The men claimed to have seen a spectral shape through the window as they sat chatting in the darkness while the rest of their platoon slept. The ghost wore a long dress and had long hair, though the face was blurred. It seemed to be angrily shouting at them. When it moved from the window towards the door, the men became convinced that it was trying to get in to do them some harm. That was why they had suddenly started shouting and hurling furniture about, actions that had awoken their comrades and caused them to think a fight was in progress.

The officer may have thought this an unlikely tale, but he was quietly told that the ghost had been seen by others. The three men were told not to make such a fuss again and were let off. It is generally thought that the ghost is that of a nurse who was raped and murdered here in the years before the Second World War.

A very odd event took place just outside Blandford in the 1660s. Baron Ryves fell asleep one summer's afternoon in his garden there. As he slept he had a remarkable dream that appeared so vivid and real that it made a strong impression and Baron Ryves wrote it down when he awoke. He dreamed that he was awake in his garden when he heard a loud rushing noise. Looking about he saw a monster as large as a small house hurtling towards him belching smoke from its head and emitting sparks and smoke from the sides of its body. The hideous creature roared past him, pulling behind it a long body. In that body were windows through which Baron Ryves could see people looking out at him. Then the monster was gone and Baron Ryves woke up.

What makes the story quite remarkable is that about 150 years later the Somerset and Devon Railway built its lines through what had been Baron Ryves' garden. And along that line ran steam engines belching smoke and sparks, pulling carriages in which sat people looking out of windows.

# BADBURY RINGS

Badbury Rings is an almost perfectly circular complex of three concentric rings of earthwork defences that tower high above the valley of the Stour. They date to the Iron Age, when Dorset and the surrounding area was ruled by the Celtic people known as the Durotriges. The towering earthen ramparts would originally have been topped by wooden palisades, lined by warriors when danger threatened. It would not have been an easy place to take, though the Romans managed to do so. The site was virtually abandoned throughout the Roman period, but was reoccupied in the turbulent times that followed the collapse of the Roman Empire. It is to this period that its ghosts are thought to belong.

The shadowy figures that are seen here are armed with the spears and round shields that are typical of the post-Roman period. Local legend has it that King Arthur once lived here, fighting the invading Saxons with determination for every acre of British soil. Some scholars believe that Badbury Rings might be the place named in chronicles over a thousand years ago as Mount Badon. The Mount has never been properly located, but it is known that Arthur fought a three-day battle against the Saxons at Badon, and that Arthur was attacking a fortified slope. This could well be Badbury, for the name and the lie of the land fit quite neatly – though it must be admitted that so do those of several

*Sheep graze peacefully on the old fortifications of Badbury Rings. The quiet here is sometimes shattered by some impressive ghosts.*

other places. Nevertheless, the presence of the ghosts indicates that something happened here.

The most dramatic manifestation of the ghosts of Badbury Rings came in summer 1970 when a group of archaeological students were camping there while undertaking a dig. All went well until one particular evening when the students' jovial evening camp meal was interrupted by some aggressive shouting from the darkness. Unable to catch quite what was being bellowed at them in such threatening terms, the students probed the darkness with torches. They could see nothing, but the shouting had been replaced by the steady tramp of feet as if hundreds of men were advancing over the grass towards them. When the sound of metal weapons clashing together was added to the renewed shouting, the students fled.

What makes the stories that surround Badbury Rings so interesting is that it is possible to trace the development of the legend. The tales of ghostly men carrying shields at Badbury are ancient indeed, but in the old stories they were not identified. It was only in 1883 that the historian Edwin Guest suggested that Badbury Rings might be the site of the battle of Mount Badon. By the 1930s the spectral figures at Badbury were being said to be linked to Arthur and in 1968 it was first definitely stated that the ghosts were King Arthur and his knights. So if the Arthurian link comes from the work of Mr Guest in the later 19th century, it leaves unanswered the question: Just whose ghosts are these?

*A ghostly Roman legionnary has been seen near to Badbury Rings.*

A few miles to the west of Badbury Rings a group of schoolboys and their teacher were confronted by a spectral Roman soldier, complete with oblong shield, short sword and helmet. The apparition was in view for several seconds before fading into nothingness. The sighting took place at Thorncombe Wood, which lies beside the old Roman road from Dorchester to Badbury Rings.

## WIMBORNE

One of Dorset's most enigmatic phantoms is to be seen beside the B3078 to the north of Wimborne Minster, close to the road junction that leads off to Clapgate. More than one person has reported seeing a coffin lying on the verge. The phantom coffin is said to be that of a farmer who committed suicide by hanging himself in a long vanished barn near here. His body was brought to this road junction for burial, since suicides were not allowed Christian burial at the time. Clearly he has not rested in peace. It is not known whether

*The welcoming café in Mill Lane that has played host to the ghostly woman of Wimborne Minster.*

the ghostly black horse that gallops wide eyed down the lane into Wimborne on nights of the new moon is connected to the coffin apparition or not.

Equally odd is the spectre that frequents the Barley Mow just to the north of Wimborne Minster itself. This takes the form of a vague black cloud that moves around the bar.

Rather more solid is the ghost of the Reverend Percy Newall, which haunts his old rectory. He is seen most often early in the morning, the good Reverend being a famously early riser, walking upstairs with a Bible in his hands.

Just as clear is the young woman who has been seen in Mill Lane. This is the ghost of Annie, a 15-year-old girl who worked at the mill which stood beside the River Allen here in the 1770s. One day, Annie came running out of the mill at top speed, tripped and fell into the mill race where she drowned. The miller denied knowing anything about it and claimed to have no idea why the girl had been so apparently terror stricken.

The girl's family, however, soon came forward to tell the authorities that young Annie had been complaining that the miller was taking an altogether unwelcome interest in her burgeoning maturity. Annie had been looking for another job at the time, and her family claimed that the only reason she would have run so rashly from the mill would have been to escape an attempted seduction or rape. Nobody could prove anything, however, so the miller went free. But the locals made certain that no more teenage girls applied for jobs at the mill.

Whatever the truth about her death, young Annie continues to haunt the area. She wanders Mill Lane in a disconsolate fashion so that several of those who see her try to offer help, only for the girl to vanish in front of their eyes. For some reason she is particularly attracted to the Riverside Café that overlooks the old mill race. 'We used to see her all the time,' reports one former member of staff of the 1990s. 'It was usually when the place was empty, you know, before we opened or after we closed. You would be setting tables or clearing up dirty plates and what have you, when suddenly there would be this woman in a long dress there. And then she was gone. Only ever saw her out of the corner of my eye, and just for a moment or two. But she was there as solid as you are.'

## LONGHAM

It is the River Stour that runs through Longham. For some reason this gentle stream has attracted a most gentle phantom with an odd affinity to gardeners.

The ghost is that of a lady in a long dress, wearing an old-fashioned bonnet of the type that has a brim pointing forward to hide the face from all except those directly in front. She does not seem to be much bother to anyone, although she has given at least one witness a serious fright when she materialised unexpectedly. During the 1970s the local newspaper featured a number of sightings of the ghost, all of them made by witnesses who were out in their gardens in the later afternoon doing a spot of weeding or other garden work. Perhaps the ghost was a keen gardener in life.

Another ghostly lady has been seen beside the A348 close to the church. Again, nobody seems to know who she is, but the ghost walks briskly beside the road before stepping out in front of oncoming traffic. More than one driver has had to slam on their brakes to avoid what they expect to be a messy accident. But the spectral lady always vanishes before contact is made.

# LYTCHETT MATRAVERS

Just east of the charming village of Lytchett Matravers lies a wood, alongside Huntick Road. There is something quite unpleasant and forbidding that lurks here, though nobody is quite sure what it is. Whatever the thing might be, it follows those unwary enough to walk this way after dark. Some report being followed by a tall, dark man with broad shoulders, others by an animal that pads along in their footsteps. Still more describe merely a feeling of deep unease. Whatever is happening, it is best not to linger.

Unlike Huntick Road, the manor house at Lytchett Matravers is no more. The original medieval fortified house burned down in the 1840s and its Victorian replacement fell victim to dry rot and neglect in the 1940s. The original house was said to have been haunted by Sir John Maltravers. This muscular knight of the 14th century owned getting on for half of Dorset, but his main claim to fame was his role in the death of King Edward II. That king was ousted from his throne by his wife Queen Isabel and her lover, Roger Mortimer, in 1327. Isabel and Roger ruled, pretending to act for the boy king Edward III, but in reality lining their own pockets from government funds. They gave Sir John Maltravers and his brother-in-law, Sir Thomas Berkeley, the job of getting rid of the old king, a task carried out in a particularly brutal fashion.

In old age Sir John came to repent his crimes. He insisted that he be buried without a tomb and that his body be laid to rest beneath the door of Lytchett Matravers church so that all who entered could walk over him. His ghost, it was said, wandered around his old home in penitent mood. Unable to find absolution for his many sins, the unquiet spirit could not rest. The destruction of the house seems finally to have laid Sir John's ghost

Still haunting the village, but rather more enigmatic, are the whispering ghosts that gather along the path that leads from the village to the church. The words can never be quite made out, though the voices are clear enough.

# Bournemouth

T he town of Bournemouth began as just a single house belonging to Lewis Tregonwell in 1810. Tregonwell was a great host and invited a steady stream of fashionable and wealthy folk to his house by the sea on a remote stretch of heathland. The location boasted a golden beach six miles long, a mild climate and

*The graveyard around the church in the Bournemouth suburb of Kinson has a ghost that may be connected to a mysterious discovery made here around the year 1905.*

impressive scenery. The place appealed so much that before long others were building holiday homes near that of Tregonwell, then a few hotels opened up and by 1840 there was a regular seaside resort in operation.

It is not surprising therefore that the ghosts of Bournemouth are rather younger than others to be found in Dorset, nor that the town cannot boast many that are seen with any frequency. That said, the Town Hall plays host to two ghosts, which may be connected. The first and more active is a soldier wearing a uniform of the First World War. He is seen in the autumn more than at other times of year, entering the building and then vanishing. The street outside plays host to a phantom horse, which waits patiently stamping its hooves. Perhaps the horse is waiting for the soldier.

The suburb of Kinson is rather older than Bournemouth itself, being a village from medieval times, and has its own ghosts. In the early part of the last century a skull was unearthed while a grave was being dug in the churchyard of St Andrew's. Such an event cannot be unusual, but what made this find noteworthy was that a dagger was driven right through the skull from above and behind. Soon afterwards the ghost of a young woman dressed in a long dress with a bustle began to be seen in and around the churchyard. She is seen still, but if she has any message to impart about the gruesome find she is keeping it to herself.

Gullivers Bar was formerly haunted by the spectre of an elderly man who would sit in the bar counting out a pile of gold coins. He has not been seen since the pub was refurbished to become a trendy, modern bar.

# POOLE

Poole is blessed with a vast natural harbour which, although too shallow for modern ocean-going ships, was for generations a safe haven for vessels of all kinds. Merchants grew rich on the trade in which their ships engaged and Poole prospered along with them. It was that maritime wealth that led to the oldest of the hauntings in the town.

In 1598 merchant William Greene passed away. He left his widow, Alice, his home at Scaplan's Court, his ships, his goods and £200 in hard cash. In those days a workman was lucky to earn £5 a year, so this was an impressive sum indeed. Among those impressed were Richard Parmiter, Robert Hill, Godwin Spencer and John Beryman, who lived next door to Scaplan's Court. Together they decided to steal the money. Their plan lacked subtlety.

As night fell on the day after William Greene's funeral, the four men went round to Scaplan's Court. They kicked the front door in and burst through. Agnes Beard, the maid, was sitting on the stairs just inside the front door eating her supper. She looked up in surprise, whereupon Robert Hill struck her on her head with an axe, killing her instantly. Hill then ran upstairs to despatch Widow Greene in similarly brutal fashion, together with her dog which was barking. Hill's accomplices seem to have been unprepared for such savagery. They turned him in and watched him hang.

It would appear to be the ghost of the unfortunate maid Agnes who haunts the building. The phantom wears a long dark dress, over which is a white apron or pinafore. She haunts the area around the staircase, often walking with determined stride up the stairs, or sometimes simply standing beside them for a few seconds before fading from view.

The Crown Hotel has no such unpleasant history, but is undoubtedly haunted. It was in the 1960s that a thorough renovation of the 300-year-old building seems to have sparked off the supernatural incidents. Up in the attic a small chamber was discovered hidden behind a wooden partition. This find at once reminded local historians of a former landlord who had been convicted of killing two of his children because they had been born disabled. The murders had followed some years of the children being hidden away in a secret chamber. If the chamber discovered in the attic had been the room where the children were imprisoned, and perhaps killed, it might explain the disturbances that followed.

Lights were switched on and off, footsteps echoed from empty rooms

*The Crown Hotel at Poole hit the headlines in the 1960s, but the ghosts here have been quiet in recent years.*

and the sounds of invisible horses stamping about in the courtyard were heard. The figure of a woman was seen upstairs and the haunting sound of a piano drifted out of the former stables. The paranormal events reached a crescendo, then faded away. Whoever, or whatever, had been disturbed by the building work soon went back to rest. Only the phantom piano playing continued to be heard. In 1989 the ghostly pianist became quite active for several weeks, but then again decided enough was enough.

These days the Crown retains its reputation for being haunted but the staff are generally more concerned with making their human visitors feel welcome. If there is a ghost, it does not bother anyone these days.

# CULPEPPER'S DISH

Culpepper's Dish is a remarkable natural formation that stands a little outside the village of Briantspuddle in the midst of a Forestry Commission plantation. Fortunately, the Commission has provided a car park for those who wish to visit.

The Dish itself is an almost perfectly round natural sinkhole, with exceptionally steep sides that dive over 50 ft down into the ground. The scramble down is rather difficult, and up again even worse so it is not really advisable to venture into the place. It is best admired from the rim.

The lane that runs past Culpepper's Dish to Briantspuddle is haunted by a phantom funeral. Four men march in unison with a coffin on their shoulders. They are heading towards Briantspuddle, but never seem to get there. They simply march endlessly past Culpepper's Dish.

A footpath runs north from the Dish over the sandy heath and between stands of pine trees. After about half a mile, the path runs along the edge of a steep hill that drops away into a marshy morass dominated by the dark, stagnant waters of Rimsmoor Pond.

This pond has an evil reputation and the path above it is haunted by a man who was unwary enough to come this way one night in the 18th century. He was a young man from Briantspuddle who was riding home late on a summer's evening. Nobody knows quite what happened to him, but he failed to reach home and next day a search party set out. They were able to follow the hoof-prints of his horse as far as the path above Rimsmoor Pond. There the sandy surface of the path was torn up as if some terrible struggle had taken place, although there were no other tracks to indicate that footpads or highwaymen had been involved. Indeed, there was just an ominous drag track heading towards the dark waters of the pond. There was no sign of either man or horse. They had simply vanished.

The ghost appears late on a summer evening, the sort of evening when the man vanished in real life. A horseman comes riding south, dressed in a tricorn hat and mounted on a bay horse. He follows the path that skirts the pond and its surrounding marshes, then trots up the slope to reach the crest of the hill. There the man stops to stare down at Rimsmoor Pond and then horse and rider vanish into thin air.

# CLOUDS HILL

C louds Hill is a popular spot for walkers, and no wonder. The lanes are quiet, while numerous footpaths run across the nearby fields and through the scenic woods. It is these walkers who have reported hearing the sound of a powerful, if old-fashioned, motorbike racing down the lane from Bovington. The sound reaches a crescendo of noise, then abruptly stops and silence returns. No motorbike is ever seen.

It is widely believed that this spectral sound is the phantom recreation of the mysterious road accident in which died Thomas Edward Lawrence, better known as Lawrence of Arabia. Lawrence had led an adventurous life before settling in his little cottage at Clouds Hill. Born in Wales and educated in Oxford, he had been in Iraq studying ancient civilisations when the First World War broke out. His fluency in Arabic gained Lawrence a job in army intelligence in the Middle East. It was in this role that in 1916 Lawrence travelled into the heart of Arabia to meet the tribal leader Emir Faisal, who was in revolt against the Turkish Empire that then ruled the area and with which Britain was at war.

Over the next two years, Lawrence combined his military training with the innate desert skills of the Arabs to inflict defeat after defeat on the Turks. The campaign opened the way for the regular British forces under General Edmund Allenby to invade from Egypt, crush the Turks and overthrow the Turkish Empire. The Arabs failed to gain national independence in the peace treaties that followed so Lawrence resigned his government posts in disgust. He later joined the RAF under an assumed name, though his real identity was soon discovered, and served quietly for ten years.

Lawrence was returning from sending a telegram at Bovington on the day he died. Two schoolboys saw him go by, heard a crash and then saw a black van speeding off in the opposite direction. Lawrence was taken to hospital, but died without regaining consciousness. The black van was never identified and while he lay dying Lawrence's home was ransacked and various papers stolen – again by persons unknown.

It was a strange and mysterious death for a man who had been so famous and who had seemed to lead a charmed life throughout the years of war. No wonder that his unquiet spirit feels the need to return, revving the engine of his Brough motorbike to a full throaty roar as he races down the lanes towards the home he will never reach.

# BOVINGTON

The Tank Museum at Bovington is one of Dorset's premier tourist attractions and with good reason. It has an unequalled collection of military fighting vehicles from the past hundred years. On the days when the tanks are started up, mock battles are fought across the open heathland with realistic explosions, gunfire and smoke. It is an event not to be missed.

Missing none of it is the ghost known lightheartedly as Herman the German. He appears dressed in the smart black uniform of a Panzer officer from the Second World War. The ghost is generally thought to be linked to the museum's Tiger Tank. This superb fighting vehicle was officially known as the Panzer VI, but was soon dubbed the Tiger by its crews.

The massive tank weighed 57 tons, but could still manage a top speed of 24 mph and could travel 140 miles without refueling. Its great strength lay in its armour and armament. The powerful 88 mm gun could knock out any tank in the world at long range when the Tiger entered combat towards the end of 1942 and remained supreme on the battlefield to the end of the war. Meanwhile, the superbly engineered

*A tank stands parked outside the Tank Museum at Bovington, where a mysterious figure has been seen ever since the establishment acquired a new exhibit.*

100 mm armour made the Tiger impervious to the guns of other tanks and anti-tank weapons unless attacked at close range from behind.

These supreme killing machines ruled the battlefields of the Second World War, being vulnerable only to close combat, air attack or a lack of fuel. It was the latter that eventually drove these monsters to defeat, but quite a few were damaged in combat. The tank at Bovington Tank Museum was one such and it is generally thought that the ghostly Herman the German was a crew member killed in battle who cannot bear to leave his beloved Tiger.

## BINDON ABBEY

There is not much left to see at Bindon Abbey, a little to the east of Wool. The agents sent by King Henry VIII in the 1540s did their work well. The abbey lands were confiscated and sold off, the buildings stripped of anything of value and the few stones that were left were abandoned to decay and neglect.

The site is not haunted by cowled monks walking slowly with measured tread, as one might imagine, but by a beautiful young woman. Dressed in a long flowing cloak, she walks from the site of the abbey down to the nearby River Frome and paces gently along the banks of the river.

A local legend has it that, back in the days of the abbey, a novice monk by the name of Luberlu encountered a beautiful maiden down by the river when out on an errand. The two fell to talking and before long Luberlu was besotted. Whenever he got the chance he volunteered for jobs that would take him down to the river meadows where he could meet the strange girl, who did not seem to belong to any of the local families. Slowly Luberlu began to neglect his studies as his mind turned away from a purely spiritual life.

The abbot tackled Luberlu and asked him why he was having second thoughts about his vocation. The boy confessed that he had fallen in love, but at first the abbot would not believe the story of the beautiful woman down by the river. He decided to follow Luberlu one day and saw him meet the object of his love. After the boy had gone back to the abbey, the abbot watched from hiding as the lovely girl wandered back to the river, slipped into the rushes and disappeared into the waters.

Confronting Luberlu with the information that his supposed love was a pagan water nymph who was seeking to suck him of his life-force to enhance her own, the abbot demanded the boy disown her. Luberlu refused and raced down to the Frome, but the girl was not there. He never found her again, so returned to his monastic life.

But the nymph has not abandoned the Frome. She is still to be seen wandering the meadows in the form of a young woman wearing a long cloak of grey or pale brown material. Whether the legend of Luberlu has any truth to it or not, the spectral figure still lingers on, waiting and waiting for someone.

A short distance to the west, near Wool, an ancient stone bridge crosses the Frome. This is the venue for the famous spectral Turbeville Coach. One of the notorious Death Coaches that frequent Dorset is said

*The ancient stone bridge over the Frome near Bindon Abbey that is haunted by the famous Turbeville Coach.*

to gallop over this bridge, bringing bad luck to those who see it. This particular phantom transport can be seen only by descendants of the local Turbeville family, fictionalised by local novelist Thomas Hardy in his novel *Tess of the D'Urbervilles*. The rest of humanity can only hear the ghostly carriage as it thunders by.

# LULWORTH

The beautiful Lulworth Cove is a popular holiday destination. The sandy beach is ideal for bathing and offers children endless sandcastle building opportunities. A small café overlooking the beach prepares magnificent bacon sandwiches, while the pubs and hotels in the village itself offer more refined fare.

But in the grim days of 1940 Lulworth Cove was a very different place. The sheltered waters and shelving beach made this an ideal place for German raiders to sneak ashore, or for the dreaded panzers to surge out of invasion barges and begin the subjugation of Britain to the will of Germany's Nazi dictator, Adolf Hitler. Alert to the threat, the British army moved quickly. The waters off the beach were mined, the beach festooned with barbed wire and sown with more mines, while machine gun nests were set up to sweep the potential landing ground with murderous fire. And finally a sentry was set to watch the cove, ready to alert the platoon of soldiers in the village if danger threatened.

One calm, moonlit night the sentry was amazed to see people down on the beach. They were dancing. No human could walk those sands and live, not with all the barbed wire and mines, and yet there were a dozen or more dancing gently around the seashore. The sentry sounded the alert, but by the time his comrades got in position the mysterious dancers had gone. The ghostly dancers of Lulworth have been seen several times since, prancing gracefully along the beach on moonlit nights. One man who anchored his yacht in the cove one night swore that he saw them walk down into the sea and vanish as they finished their dance.

The road that leads inland from Lulworth Cove to West Lulworth is haunted by the victim of a crime that was committed in the 18th century. At that time Lulworth Cove was a busy little port through which goods were brought to and from the farming communities in the area. Early one morning, in the hope of robbing some merchant of his wealth, a highwayman held up a coach making its way down to the beach. Instead he found himself attacked by the coach driver. In the brief fight that followed the coachman had his head severed by the highwayman's sword. The headless figure of the unfortunate man has been seen driving his coach down to the beach several times, but only at dawn when a chill grey light creeps over the hills.

In December 1678 Captain John Lawrence was coming home from Lulworth to Creech. He was riding along the lane past East Lulworth when he saw on the hills high above him a large body of marching men. Surprised, Lawrence stopped to watch. The men were marching north-east in ranks and the weak evening winter sun glittered off metal

*The beach at Lulworth Cove is a famous tourist attraction, but it is also home to some enigmatic ghostly dancers.*

weapons. There were at least 5,000 men in sight, probably more. Lawrence had some experience as a soldier serving in continental armies, so he knew what he was seeing.

Alarmed, Lawrence spurred his mount to raise the alarm at Wareham. Having called out the local militia, he sent a messenger on to London to warn King Charles II of the invasion. The South Bridge at Wareham was fortified, and all boats taken to the north bank of the Frome so that the advancing army would have no easy means of crossing. Soon 300 militiamen were on parade in the town, waiting to face the French, Spanish or whatever foreign army had dared invade England.

They waited in vain, for no army ever came into sight. Lawrence had been just another witness to the Phantom Army of the Purbeck Hills (other sightings are described under Kimmeridge and Corfe Castle).

# KIMMERIDGE

I t was some time in the 1680s that a smuggler was landing a small cargo of French brandy on the sands of Worbarrow Bay to the west of Kimmeridge. History does not record if he had been betrayed or if it was mere chance that brought a troop of revenue men to the bay on this particular night. Come they did, however, and it was an unlucky night for the smuggler.

According to the official story, the smuggler opened fire and was killed in the fighting that followed. The story enacted by the haunting, however, is quite different. The phantom smuggler appears on moonlit nights running along the edge of the sea in obvious panic. Reaching the far end of the bay, where a sheer cliff offers no way out, the ghostly man turns to plunge into the sea. There he starts to scream as if being struck by missiles or bullets. With blood-curdling yells of agony the ghost turns and writhes, then falls silent and slips out of sight beneath the waves.

If the behaviour of the ghost is to be believed, the smuggler did not die in a fight, but was shot down while trying to flee. These days, Worbarrow Bay lies within an army tank range, so few people visit the area and it is probably for this reason that the ghostly smuggler has not been seen recently.

Overlooking Worbarrow Bay from the west, and standing just outside the army ranges, is Bindon Hill. In AD 43 the Roman army invading Britain came here to capture a noted stronghold of the local Durotriges tribe of Celts. There does not seem to have been much fighting, so it may be that the Durotriges abandoned the site in the face of the armed might of Rome. Whatever happened, a detachment of legionnaires was left here to keep an eye on the locals and stop them reoccupying the hilltop and its earthwork fortifications. One foggy night, the Celts did return. But they did not come to fight. Instead they lured the Romans into launching a precipitate charge down a slope that led to the cliffs. The luckless Romans tumbled down the increasingly steep slope and over the edge to their deaths.

Ever afterward the Romans have periodically marched over Bindon Hill, heading north-east back towards their base. Locals were always adamant that on such nights, dogs would cower indoors and game would lie low and prove impossible to catch. It is, at any rate, one more version of the Phantom Army of the Purbeck Hills (see Lulworth and Corfe Castle for more details).

One famous visit by the Phantom Army to Bindon Hill came in 1940, when Britain was living in imminent fear of a German invasion. Daylight hours saw the brave men of the RAF fighting the Battle of Britain far overhead, but night-time brought patrols and sentries along the south coast nervously scanning the waters of the English Channel for signs of a Nazi invasion fleet. It was one such sentry on duty on Bindon Hill who encountered the Phantom Army.

He was sitting at his post, gazing south over the Channel when he heard the steady tramp of marching men approaching. The man knew his relief was not yet due, and in any case it sounded as if an entire regiment was approaching, not just a few men. As the men came closer, the sentry could make out the sounds of metal chinking on metal as if weaponry and belts were knocking together as the men moved. Then he heard a cough and some murmuring voices. Judging the approaching force to be only a few yards away, the man stood up and looked around. The bare hillside was empty of men and a sudden silence fell on the place. He was alone.

# KINGSTON

K ingston is one of the larger villages on the Isle of Purbeck. It stands on a hilltop that offers magnificent views north to Corfe Castle and west to the huge natural amphitheatre known locally as the Golden Bowl. The church here was not built until 1874, but is a masterpiece by the Victorian architect George Street, who went on to design the Law Courts in London and to train William

Morris and Philip Webb.

The ghost at Kingston is to be found at the Scott Arms pub, which faces the church across West Street. The pub itself is a welcoming place serving delicious home cooked meals. The phantom is that of an elderly lady who is seen sometimes pottering through the bar as if searching for something. Obviously she never finds it for she vanishes, only to reappear again some months later.

*The ghost of the Scott Arms prefers the older part of the building, being seen most often in the front bar of the pub.*

The phantom is reportedly that of the lady who owned the place when it was the village shop. Metal hoops in the ceiling behind the bar show that the area was once a larder where local game was hung before being sold. A photograph of the lady in question also hangs behind the bar. 'That's her,' said the barman in 2006, 'clear as day that is her. She potters about the front bar mostly, that was her shop you see. But sometimes she is seen round the back, though not often. We don't see her for more than a moment or two. She is always walking quickly as if she is in a rush to get somewhere, you see. So she is out of sight almost before you realise it is her. But it is that old girl, all right. No doubt. I've seen her myself.'

# Corfe Castle

The village of Corfe Castle owes its name to the mighty fortress which dominates the area from the hill overlooking the road to Swanage. It was that road which, indirectly, led to the more active of the hauntings at Corfe Castle.

*The magnificent ruins of Corfe Castle dominate the countryside for miles around and harbour a number of phantoms.*

During the English Civil War, the Bankes family, which owned the castle and surrounding lands, were loyal to the king. Sir John Bankes and most of the menfolk rode off to serve in the army of King Charles I against the forces of Parliament. Lady Bankes was left to hold Corfe Castle with a small garrison. At first all went well. The serious fighting was miles away and only an occasional Roundhead patrol ventured onto the Bankes's lands.

By 1645 the situation had changed. Most of southern England was firmly in the hands of the Roundheads, with only Corfe holding out. And Corfe was proving to be a strategic site. The castle and its garrison could effectively close Swanage, then a major port, by blocking the road inland. Parliament could no longer tolerate such a situation, so an army was sent to take Corfe Castle.

Although Corfe was an old medieval castle, its position was naturally impregnable and no matter which modern engine of war the Parliamentarians put into action, the defences stood firm. It was not until February 1646, when food was running out and the garrison faced starvation, that Colonel Pitman betrayed his employer, Lady Bankes, and opened the gates to the enemy.

Lady Bankes was treated relatively well by the standards of the day, but her mighty fortress was first confiscated and then blown up with gunpowder. The massive ruins that remain stand pretty much as they were when the army of Parliament marched away and give some clue as to the past glories of the fortress. It is no wonder that Lady Bankes, who held her home for her king for so long, should return in spectral form. She is seen most often walking outside the main walls of the castle, gliding gently down to the stream that runs around the foot of the hill on which the castle stands. She walks with her head bent forward and with stately tread. Perhaps she tries to recreate the long years of happiness that she knew there.

The fortress of Corfe Castle stands on the easternmost spur of the Purbeck Hills. Running along the crest of the hills is a broad green track that drops down to the lowlands in front of the castle. It is along this track that the famous Phantom Army of Purbeck has been seen marching. The army is usually said to be that of Roman legionaries pounding their way over the upland road that they used in life, and other sightings are described under Lulworth and Kimmeridge.

# STUDLAND

Above Studland lies an expanse of heathland, across which a track runs to Shell Bay, near the mouth of Poole Harbour. The area of open woodland and scrubby gorse is variously known as Newton Heath or Studland Heath, but the ghost that lurks there has no name at all.

It was in about 1802, when the wars with Napoleonic France were at their height, that a man from Studland visited relatives at an isolated farm on the southern shores of Poole Harbour. It was a few days before Christmas and the man knew he would be returning late and, possibly, the worse for wear. So, he took with him his white donkey to help him get home again safely.

Unfortunately, also out on the heath that night was a deserter from the Royal Navy in desperate need of a means of making a quick getaway. When the drunken fisherman came in sight mounted on his white donkey, the deserter saw an opportunity. A donkey was no horse, but it was better than nothing. He ambushed the fisherman, but drunk or not the man was able to put up a stiff fight. By the time the deserter had rendered his victim unconscious, the donkey was gone and nowhere in sight. The deserter fled, but was soon caught. Since the fisherman had died of exposure through being left unconscious on the heath, the hapless deserter was hanged for murder.

That left the white donkey as something of a mystery for it was never found, at least not alive. It returns in spectral form to haunt the heath, being seen most often in December, or in the few days after Christmas. The ghost does nothing more threatening than munch at the grass, but it can give witnesses a sudden shock when it vanishes in an instant.

The village of Studland itself is said to be haunted by the unquiet spirit of a smuggler. This unfortunate fellow was murdered sometime in the 1780s when storing a large consignment of costly silks in his cottage on behalf of the gang to which he belonged. Nobody was ever convicted of the crime and it was this that was thought to have caused the smuggler's ghost to walk. The figure of the seafaring man with a blue jacket and red scarf around his neck does not seem to have put in an appearance of recent years, so perhaps he has finally found rest.

One strange phenomenon that continues is that of the singing sands of Studland. An unearthly moaning or humming sound sometimes booms out from the sands along the coast near here. Scientists would have us believe it is caused by the grains of sand rubbing against each other when the wind or tide are in just the right position, but the old stories record that these are the sounds of the souls of those shipwrecked along the coast, crying out for a decent Christian burial.

# •Index•